The Way of Doe:

journal of a near-holywoman

the way of Doe:
journal of a near-holywoman

Mesa Doe

NEAR-HOLYtm BOOKS

Near-Holy Press

Printed in the United States of America.

Designed by Sharon Fernleaf / Near-Holy Press

"Guru Goodies" is a trademark of Sharon Fernleaf.
"Near-Holy", "nearholy" and Near-Holy Books" are trademarks of Sharon Fernleaf.

ISBN 0-9703629-0-0 Print version
ISBN 0-9703629-1-9 Electronic version
Library of Congress Control Number   2001118214

This book is dedicated to my beloved mother, Hazel;
to Sherri, my brilliant life partner; and to the
love of my life—Nina Rae, my daughter.

Acknowledgements
I'm grateful for everything, but here are a few special mentions:

Sister Melody, one of the most spiritual people I have the honor of knowing; Dawn, little sister; Justin; Cody; Ashley; Elizabeth; Sue Smith; Betty Krier; Dick Smith; Barb Meier; Mrs. Duke; Steve Fidel; Barry McNabb; David Downing; Ms. Magazine; Rubyfruit Jungle; the University of Oregon; Jean Eckstrom; Olga Broumas; the lesbian community of Eugene, Oregon; Kari Hodgson and family. Riva Wolvek and her ranch in Twisp, the Methow Valley of Washington; Yolanda, eagle feathers and motherworks. Margaret Lawrence; Janice Gutman; PJ; Peggy Pullen and Jamie Lee; Anne Miller; Artemis; Jasper; Bette Lamont; Linda Gryczan; Visions; the lesbian community of Seattle, Washington; and an extraordinary psychic—Martha Equinox. Kelli and her website in Arkansas; TC, medicine man in Seattle; Mona Bachmann, always, and new forms/few norms; Laura Van Dommelen and family; Rocky and Sugar; Janie Winder and family in Pennsylvania; Boo Boo and Pookie; Judith Rosen, my dear friend in Igo, California; Janet Dietrich; Penny Mock; Rick, Barb Boaz, Joanie, and Steve, etc...of YCC in Sandy, Oregon; Pat, the minister from Kalamazoo; K.D. and Carter in Hamilton, Montana; Maryann the psychic geneticist in Missoula; the exceptionally friendly people in Oklahoma City; Dennis and Janine at Whataburger; Lauren the artist and her beloved three legged dog in Cape Cod; Guillermina-Giron Stein, the Teacher I honor the most, without having told her; Renee Mazon and Dorothy Holden in New Mexico; Michael (Matthew) Groves—chef extraordinaire in Albuquerque; Tori, the naturopath; Melanie Kaye-Kantrowitz, Adrienne Rich, and Sinister Wisdom; Carol Burton; Elaine Hall; Johno; and the Oregon women's community in 1978; art history/design professor, Donna ;Lee Jacobson, sculptor and professor at Chemeketa, where this book was begun; Stephanie and her phone booth in Boston; Donna Kramer, the hilarious in Brooklyn; and Apollonia; Zoe; Yama; Jordan; Kafkaesque; beloved Gabriella, the divine; Rumitilda, the magnificent; Tai, the beautiful heart; and Sam, the lovely little boy. Thanks for everything.

The Lesson

"Love the hell out of yourself."

(If you practice on yourself before letting loose
on the general public, you might first get the kinks
worked out and do less damage later.)

—Mesa Doe
(Near-Holywoman)

Introduction

I, Mesa Doe, am beloved.

I have to believe this because I based an entire transformation on this assumption, and believe me, don't bother asking anyone else, it was pretty impressive. I have recorded my entire process for the benefit of expected future followers, who will, no doubt, go digging around in my past, looking for God/dess knows what—so here, I am giving them the real goods.

This journal is also for me. In case I am ever hit on the head, rendering me more senseless, and abandoned by memory (God/dess knows what a drag it is to repeat lessons ad infinitum, and what a rare occurrence as well...) In addition, this document holds the promise of endless party entertainment: when someone asks, "Did you know_____? (fill in the blank), I can whip out my journal and say with certainty, "Yes, yes, I did know. And I knew on this date. When exactly did you know?" (This works best when at a party of people not quite as bright as myself, or at least, did not arrive at their knowledge before I did. If this is not the case and the group is pretty sharp, I'm hanging with the wrong crowd. And unless the food is spectacular, I leave. I like others to grow to my level, not the other way around. (I have a small problem with humility, but this small blemish on my character keeps me in close rapport with the masses.)

Throughout this entire process of transformation, I have come to believe completely in the idea of perpetual motion, like it or not. I tried to go back to the familiar again and again, but the womb is welcoming just that one time. Now, I am taking aim and trying to shoot my arrow of truth into the world without impaling anyone, including myself. (I use the word "aim" loosely and with a great deal of blind faith.)

Once I realized that I was truly loved—by the planet, the Universe, God/dess—I felt pretty safe loving myself. I mean, I knew I had something pretty good to fall back on.

Loving myself became a fun thing and led to a joyful rebirth, (spiritual writing requires that we wax a bit poetic) following a passionate encounter with my Higher Self—the One Who Creates; Divinity. I discovered love, passion, and creativity; seeing they were only One—Divinity. Divinity the only foundation for building; the only license to create.

And I had, without knowing, envisioned Her as my future self.

Before birth, when I was still spirit and hanging out among the stars, being happy, I know I had this great plan for my upcoming life on Earth. There was room for spontaneity, but I had a basic blueprint like everyone else. We have these, you know, like, "I will create sliced processed cheese and it will have a major impact on society." And that it did. Or, "I will liberate the world from bondage by sacrificing myself on behalf of all humanity and it will have a major impact on society." And that it did, with striking similarity to the advent of sliced processed cheese.

So, like all other humans before and after, I had a plan; a mission, when I came in. And like everyone else, when I finally arrived, I left it all behind; blueprint, memory, the whole thing. Still, throughout my life, I have felt there was something I was supposed to do here, on the planet. I've had a sense of mission; helping to save the world or something--

A "Calling".

(Okay, a pretty clear Calling.)

(Note: A calling almost always comes just as you have given up any hope of finding purpose in your life, but don't let this encourage you to give up too quickly or easily. Forget I even mentioned it.)

Author's Note

I was destined for greatness.

"Mesa, you have a lot to offer the world, the least of which is love and understanding."

--Mrs. Earl

(high school art teacher)

Since graduating, those words have given me strength and faith more times than I care to say. In gratitude to Mrs. Earl, ten years later, I wrote back, thanking her for the gift. She promptly replied, "Mesa, to tell you the truth, I had to look you up in the yearbook to remember who you were."

(Note: Magnanimity is a facial tic in the scheme of things. It passes.)

Welcome to my life...

One

I was right in the middle of a jumbo bag of Cheetohs when it happened. First Saul on the road to Damascus and now me, Mesa Doe, in front of the TV, watching Cagney and Lacey, when out of the gray: transformed.

Sitting in an old used to be yellow sofa, a rusty spring up my backside, leafing through a study bible given me by a born-again Christian on my baptism two years prior. I had not received this protection as a child and sought it as an adult. Be careful who you get to do this for you—clear any past problems the two of you might have had.

This bible, with a thorough index and interpretations for nearly every passage contained within, was a flash of brilliance on her part, since she wanted me to join the ranks of Christendom. She thought, I am sure, that I might eventually read the entire thing as I found more and more subjects in the index that directly related to my own life and problems. She never came right out and called me self-centered. I considered that a small kindness.

So, there I was, sitting on my old brown sofa, turning pages in clumps of two and three hundred, leaving pollen-like smears of orange Cheetoh in the corners—a useful thing; bringing those pages to attention later when, like now, I was desperately seeking random guidance. Then there it was.
The answer to "what am I doing here, really?"

"God chose the foolish things of the world to shame the wise; God chose the weak of the world to shame the strong. God chose the lowly things of this world and the despised things and the things that are not—to nullify the things that are, so that no one may boast before Him." --1 Co. 27:29

I had been called all those things in my life: foolish, weak, lowly, and been despised by many. I had thought myself an outcast; untouchable, and I'd been right. What I had not known was the higher purpose for which I suffered.

Yet, I had also spent most of my life pleading to a higher power a case of what was, to me, my obvious specialness. And God/dess throughout had gone to great lengths to assure me that this idea was absolutely without foundation. Until today--April 15, 1985. I have found my Calling.

I have been put on this planet to shame my betters.

Two

Following the Call
(make sure you really heard something.)

Spiritual people pray and meditate a lot, so I went right over and turned off the TV—really gave this prayer thing a go. It was even great for about ten minutes. I felt incredibly inspired—just filled with purpose. On my knees in front of the TV, with my left leg gone numb all the way up to the butt, then getting tired of humbling myself where no one could see, turning the TV back on, I thought, "I'll just give God/dess a little time to think this thing over and get back to me."

God/dess did get back to me and pretty fast. I was still watching TV three hours later, making a huge effort to be receptive, when this program came on featuring a woman who channeled some kind of being from beyond who evidently had a lot of time on his hands because he went on forever...I think waiting for the stuff to make sense to someone. I didn't understand a thing, but this woman was interesting because when she was full of this other being, she seemed happy. Actually, the other people on the show seemed happy too. They must have known something. New Age people do seem awfully happy—always getting together in groups, throwing seminars, etc...which are great, if you can afford to get into them. Evidently, the New Age will start in the best neighborhoods.

(Note: prosperous thought is easiest if you already have disposable income. Or collateral. If you are stone broke, it's called faith.)

The important thing I got from this program was they knew something about spirituality that I did not and they seemed particularly happy with what they knew. Plus, they were willing to share it on tapes and everything... I was broke so I could not get the tapes, but I knew there was a New Age bookstore down the street—a hotbed of spiritual possibility. I could walk down there and hang around for awhile, browse through a few books, soak up the atmosphere and maybe even some free-floating info from the people there. It seemed an okay place to start.

I even thought I might meet a Teacher or Guru there.

Spiritual people usually have a Guru or something. Someone who knows more than they do. I probably had one waiting for me too. Maybe even at this bookstore. Maybe that is why it occurred to me. The Teacher, my Guru, was most likely expecting me. They know these things in advance. That's why they are the Teacher and we are not.

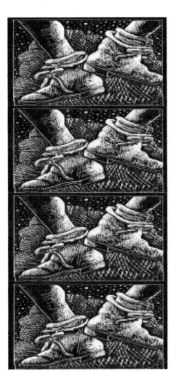

I left my house—a big deal for me. The world is not my favorite reality. Walking the three blocks up the street, it took a supreme effort to put a "profound-but-not-without-levity" expression out there on my face so my predestined Teacher would recognize me. I had practiced this face in the mirror for hours and it looked pretty good. I would have picked me out if I was looking for a student.

I walked into IT'S ALL IN YOUR MIND and heard drumming. People were looking kind of tranced out as they walked by without making any noise, which I really hated—sneaking up on me, scaring the hell out of me, making me look like a total neurotic. Then they would smile in this

irritating way, like, "Gee, someone has not found their inner peace yet, have they?" I don't mean to sound paranoid.

I spent most of my time in the "Create Your Own Reality" : Beginner's Section, which mostly contained information geared toward staying out of jail. Everyone else was in the Advanced Section, with all the money-making tips.

I had this weird feeling that messages were being directed at me, you know, subliminally, under the music, about being happy or not shoplifting or something. It was making me tense. And I couldn't afford to buy anything, so it must have been obvious that I didn't have my abundance thing together either. The pressure was killing me. If it weren't for this Teacher I was expecting, I'd have left, but I hung around for a couple of hours, waiting for my Guru to show. I was ready. I really felt like I was ready. Where was He or She? Maybe this was a test, this waiting. Faith? Patience? Stupidity? Thank God/dess I hadn't told anyone.

I finally walked home alone, passing a grocery store on the way where I picked up some chocolate and pondered my failure to find a Teacher. The wind felt great, though, blowing my hair all over my face, playing around. I would try to get out more often.

(Note: I was probably so close to enlightenment that a Teacher would be superfluous.)

As I've said, I'd always had this sense of mission. Like I was supposed to save the world. And I'd been willing to do that, as long as it did not entail leaving my house. I had been afraid to leave my house. I thought at one time that I had agoraphobia, but that wasn't it. It was the people in those big open places, so I chose not to go outside.

I did crave wide open spaces with no people in them. I had nothing against people—it wasn't about that. It was more about having the space to come up against myself. Anyway, because of this, I made of my house a hermitage; a community of myself, for six years. And community can be nurturing, supporting and embracing until the hold becomes overtight and you can no longer breathe.

In hindsight, I would have left my house sooner had I noticed the scenery was looking pretty familiar, but I actually believed I was continually walking new ground in the search for myself. Perhaps I lacked a true sense of direction, but you would be amazed at the number of ways there are to walk around your house—and before you even approach the front door.

Anyway, there was no answer in the bookstore. No Teacher. Just more frustration. Total ignorance regarding the exact nature of my purpose here. I had the big picture, now I wanted some details. And of course, God/dess in its superior wisdom and absolute refusal to be softened by any amount of begging or bribery, was not forthcoming.

Okay...so I would figure out this life thing myself, yet again. Self-reliance is a good thing, I guess, but I bet a lot of people, most, become self-reliant only after gutting the hell out of all other options first. And there is no shame in thoroughness, really.

So, so, so...the bookstore was a wash. No Teacher. No explanation. Nothing. I owed it to myself not to give up too early on this quest. I would get some kind of sign that I was on the right track.

Plan B:

I tried lots of disciplines I had read about or seen on TV
that were supposed to help me "be-at-one-with-Spirit". I
was late in the afternoon by now, so I had to do it fast, try
fast, try different things, to see what might fit.

I didn't have a bed of nails to lay on—you know, you sit there, or
lie there and focus on your navel or something, so instead, I
poured tacks and paperclips on the carpet, turned on MTV for
background music to meditate by, and sat down.

That lasted three minutes. MTV was playing boring music (it
could have been my position) and a tack had stuck right on the
callous of my big toe, making it impossible to meditate on anything
but that. Not to mention the stupid paperclips stuck to my legs
when I stood up. I spent at least an hour and a half picking them
out of the carpet and off my legs and butt.

Then I remembered Gandhi. He always wore this sheet thing, a
loincloth, and fasted a lot. I found a sheet with little baby
animals on it stuffed in my closet, so I tried wrapping it around
myself, but it was a fitted sheet. If I lived in India, the
untouchables would have crossed the street to avoid me.
I thought of chanting, but didn't know any—I did remember some

cheers from high school, but the sentiments were pretty violent.
Fasting as a possibility was completely ignored. I eat, therefore,
I really am.

I was worn out from all of this seeking after spirit, so I just took a
hot bath and went to bed.

Three

I woke up to Lao Tzu putting her paw on my cheek.
She's my Siamese cat companion, and she was lying so close to
my face that I was flattening her fur every time I exhaled. She
startled most of what was left of post-dream stuff back to
wherever it had come from. All I could hang onto were these
words, in a woman's voice:

"Woman, get thee out of the Land of Obnoxia. Then make
haste to the Wilderness."

"The Land of Obnoxia?" I asked.
"Civilization," answered the small voice in my head.
"Wilderness?" I asked.
"Virgin Territory," said the voice.
"Oh. Okay," I said.

I let the Universe boss me around quite a bit. Its batting average is much better than my own, but leave civilization? How? When I close the door against anything in the world that hurts me and I am in there alone, I still come out bruised. How do I take a trip and leave myself behind? Anyway, a trip through the Land of Obnoxia, into the Wilderness, in search of a new land. Hey ho, here I go. (Mesa Doe, brave soul.)

That is how I decided to go to the desert for a few days. Many spiritual giants have done it in the past. I could give it a shot. Jesus went for forty days and forty nights. I might make it through a weekend. Maybe.

I am going because some voice in a dream told me to and I have nothing better or more interesting to do. I think I need to get as clear as possible, so I can deal with all of the great stuff God/dess intends to bless me with. I will even die if necessary (I just want to be cooperative in case someone who really matters up there is listening and can give me a break once I am out in the middle of nowhere.)

About getting clear—to get there, you have to empty. It follows that a lot of crap is going to be released into the world. So, to me, the desert seems ideal—no one around but me. The heat will make me sweat, get dirty, and real cranky. Meaning, my personal crap should be released into the world pretty quickly.

Getting out of the Land of Obnoxia and finding virgin territory will be a challenge. I haven't been a virgin for a long time—will I recognize it? I wonder if I can find my way, not back, but through, into a New Land. Wherever and whatever that is.

I will try to keep an accurate account of the internal workings because it is important to be somewhat familiar with the mechanics of yourself when you want to do anything from fine-tuning to a major overhaul—which is what I am expecting God/dess to do out there. In my case, I am probably gutting the whole thing (me), and if I keep track of the process, and I somehow get lost, my guts will be accounted for and I'll be okay.

So, okay, before leaving, some details. I begged my neighbor Sammy to keep Lao Tzu and he promised he would if he could call her something other than Lao Tzu. According to Sammy, as a kid he had a negative run in with Chinese food. He gives few details, but I guess it was ugly. To this day, anything reminding him of this trauma causes him gastrointestinal distress. I told him, "You can probably call her anything you like as long as you feed her and give up most of your bed."

"Really?" he asked. "I can call her anything?
Lucifer..Lucifer..come here."

And she did.

Sammy set a bowl of tuna on the floor and she acted like she
had been living with him forever. Cat loyalty aside, there were
other matters. I thought about giving up my apartment. Call me
crazy, but why not a giant leap of faith? My life could change
when I go to the desert. I might be utterly transformed. It could
happen. What could also happen, I could die, so why pay rent?
Or I could nearly die and need to come home to recuperate and
have no apartment to come home to. Really, faith is one of those
things that takes some planning. I'd wait on the giant leap.

I packed an old green army pack, feeling an equal measure of
fear and excitement. My joints were achy from a gallon of
coffee. I knew it was the coffee because I had just read a book
on the hazards of caffeine. (Note: if you are going to destroy
your body, make it destruction borne of education, not
ignorance. This way, you at least appear to be in control of
your lack of control. I try to stay abreast of things.)

Then I panicked. What if I couldn't eat for a long time? "It'll be
good for you," said a voice that sounded like mine but could not

have been because I would never say anything like that.
"There's nothing here to eat anyway..so let's hit the road,"
urged the voice. True, the cupboards were bare.
Good time to leave. "We're out of here," I said, more
confidently than I felt, but it worked. I walked out the door in
hopes of a grand adventure. It could beat the hell out of TV
and Cheetohs.

Maybe. We would see.

The
JOURNAL

GURU GOODIE:
Take yourself out of context every once in awhile, to see who you are on your own.

Day One:

On the road to wilderness

" Jesus, full of the Holy Spirit, returned from the Jordan and was led by the spirit in the desert, where forty days he was tempted by the devil."
Luke 4:1-2

"There are small, gentle dunes in all directions, like a young girl's budding breasts. Is this virgin territory? (What a joke...virgins aren't gentle. They are voracious and imprecise. Never mind. That was a long time ago.)
Mesa Doe

I want a hamburger. There is no way in hell I would do this for forty days. I cannot believe I brought all of this stuff with me. I'm walking along the road, on my way to the middle of nowhere, and I'm carrying a house on my back. I mean, why leave home, for crying out loud? The idea of dropping everything, shoving it all under something, is just too tempting, so I do. Or at least most of it. I keep the pack, the water and notebooks. I have to trust that what I need and don't have will either come to me or I will be led to it. Or neither. I don't care. It's too damned heavy.

No food. No coffee. No cigarettes. No sugar, no music, no TV. Nothing to read and no one to talk to. Well, that part is okay, at least for a while. No bed, no clean clothes, and no bath. Oh, that'll make me crazy. I hope I don't start to smell. I think wild animals like that sort of thing.

There is a raven sitting on top of an ancient gatepost across the road and she laughs as she flies away, off over sand and sage, small dunes spread out behind the gate. My eyes follow her as she moves beyond distant orange hills. I walk on when I can no longer hear her laughter, in a pretty pissy mood, actually. I wonder if Jesus felt this way. Think about it. Forty days and nights without food, water, or anything, and the devil too. Could piss a person off, really. I feel cranky and tired of walking so I'm stopping. It's beginning to get too hot, but I refuse to let this mood ruin everything. I'm not getting off to an unpleasant start here. Just in case anyone in the divine realms is paying attention. There is absolutely no one else around, not one human, and this is truly exciting. Solitude is good. I'm stripping off my clothes and surveying my place. I know, humans are so territorial, but at least I didn't go around peeing on everything. Words are much more civilized. So, what I see is mine, while I am here. And I'm pleased by the sand and sun, low mountains way out there, the underfed clouds pushed across the blue-white sky, just like dust on the lip of a broom. Brooms don't really have lips, I'm just feeling kind of poetic. Really, at this moment, I don't know what all the fuss has been about. This is great. No problem. Jeez, I want to dance and no one is around. No music either. Only this song in my heart. Woman is truly mistress of all she surveys.

You know, I have not felt this good in, I don't know, I don't think I have ever felt this good.

I've always wanted to be an eagle. Or a dolphin. Or anything, I guess. Anything else. And while no one is here, I can be anything I want. Maybe grow some feathers and dance around like an eagle possessed. (Interlude: dance of the possessed eagle. Five minutes. A glorious thing I wish someone could have seen.)

The sand is too damned hot. I'm putting my shoes back on. Hey! I'm going to have a major tan! I hadn't even thought of that. I will be enlightened and have no bikini line. I know I should not care about that sort of thing, but while I am maybe getting closer to perfection, I can look good.

Maybe I'll come back to the world and start a new religion. Maybe I'll be an evangelist. Now, they have great tans. They've probably spent a great deal of time wandering the desert, seeking guidance. Maybe in Palm Springs.

There is nothing in spiritual writings I've ever read that specifically commands we not look good. And I think the key in dealing effectively with vanity is in not worrying about how we look, and I do not, as long as I look okay. Then I stop thinking about it until I no longer look okay. I'm sure that's pretty normal. Actually, I don't care. I really need to eat. I could be an evangelist, you know, wear white, especially after my stay here, make my tan stand out, but making sure to have some kind of stain in plain view so as not to distance myself from the People. It's now too hot to be running around. I need to find a cool spot somewhere to lie down for a while. Like under a rock.

Three hours and a gallon of sweat later, I hear a voice on the wind.

"There is no enemy," it says. I am laying alone here, in the fetal position, in the shade of a rock, in the middle of a desert. I close my eyes and think I hear drums. An image begins to form behind my eyes. I see my future self—the me I will be when I am truly happy. Walking down a street, anonymous, among hundreds of people and cars. The image is foggy, but coming together. Everything is in slow motion. The drums I thought I heard are hundreds of feet falling around me as we all walk down a crowded street. It looks like New York—really big. And in great cinematic fashion, there is a killer soundtrack happening with this imagery.

There is a big canvas bag draped across my chest. Boy, I look strong. I'm impressed. Wonder how that happened. I pull an apple out of the bag, take a bite and walk into Central Park—up some stairs to a stage that's been prepared for something important. There is a diffuse light around my head and hands, and faint stars dance around me in space. I understand that I am an internationally known healer, so I see that it is me that's important. How fun. I take off my shades and people start rushing the stage, climbing up to get to me. They all want me to heal them, or sign an autograph. Then slowly, I am getting shoved further into the crowd, closer to the edge of the stage.

Things are in a bit of an uproar and no one notices that I am no longer in the center of the stage. In fact, I have just fallen backwards off of it. I am lying on the ground in a heap and some guy is standing on my hand, my holy hand.

I guess I don't have to hurt myself, even in vision, just to make a point, that being, people sometimes want to be healed, but the healer doesn't matter, not really, beyond being physical and serving as some kind of proof or testimony—you know, something that can be pointed to when explaining the miracle, since they don't see God/dess.

When I open my eyes, I am still here in the desert, alone, in case I forgot to mention that before. Still, the breeze is pretty intimate. On the hot sand, I have to tell myself that the burning against my skin is a sensation, like any other—it will pass, a stranger, if I don't get too familiar with it. And now, there is sand up my nose and in my left ear—an interesting feeling. Having nothing better to do, I watch the little crystals dance across one another as I exhale. I am waiting. I am...I I I iiiii am already getting bored with myself. It's good to know it's possible, not so good maybe, that it happened so fast. I'm hungry, though my head feels too full. "Look! Over there! " I said, louder than necessary, there being no one around to hear. I got up and walked toward it. "Jeez, it's just a candy wrapper." I fondle it just the same.

Everything out here is flat, but the far hills and the delicate dunes and the air moving in waves, like an elemental Salome. Something pale yellow, far away, off to my right. There is nothing else, so I go over there. It is so small and alone there, moving slightly, touched by the air. It's a flower, shaped like a small cup. Its petals are pale and crumpled, like orphaned tracing paper. The leaves are dark and narrow, long and look very strong. The sand around the flower is folded in waves and the flower is on the crest of the largest. I don't know why I'm moved by this, but it makes no sense it being here. I think about uprooting it, taking it with me, but where am I going? I wait, while the air moves around my skin, and I give slightly to its touch. I'm so hungry. It's been hours since I ate anything. Boy, I will make a great spiritual leader—sacrifice comes so easily to my nature. Oh well, I do have visions. Have since I was a kid. That counts for something. I mean, I think it's a prerequisite for spiritual giants, and it is certainly expected if you are in the middle of a desert for any length of time. I remember my first vision.

It was 1963. I was six.

My First Vision:
(I'll try to announce the big things, so no one is caught off guard
by wondrous phenomena...)

I am alone in the dark of my bedroom, dancing in circles on the
bed, singing with the hundreds of stars and planets cascading
from my fingers out into space, when the air around me tingles
and raises the hair on my arms. Then I see them. The white
outline of a man, an outline only—there is no inside to speak of.
And the pale light in the shape of a ball, like a beach ball, rolling
in space at the left side of my bed.

They moved slowly around the bed, the beachball rolling along,
level with the man's left shoulder. I am not afraid, but I stare at
them and they make their way around, all the way up to the right

side where I stand on a pillow. Then the man asks me, "Mesa, will you be eternally powerful?"

I couldn't really answer the question and hoped it was merely rhetorical, but at least I knew they meant me no harm; my body was pretty calm, almost happy, except for the nausea. So, I knew they were okay, but I didn't know how to answer them. Maybe I'd be powerful. Maybe not. I just did not know yet. I do know that the next morning I tied my own shoes without help or whining, so I guess a choice on power had been made.

Power has been a major theme in my life: what it is, how to get it, do I even want it and what to do with it once I do have it? And gypsies. I always go back to gypsies. A year before my first vision, when I was five, we lived with gypsies in Sacramento, California. My mother was with this gypsy named Johnny. He and his brother, who lived next door, made outdoor furniture. That picnic stuff people have in their backyards and we see in the state parks, painted green.

Anyway, I had long black hair and dark skin and Johnny's niece was my age and we looked like twins. We would stay outside all day, dancing around a big fire, to the sound coming out of a little black radio. We would blast the music through a thick haze of sawdust air. "My Boy Lollipop" was always on, it seemed. And we'd run to the end of the dirt driveway everyday at noon to buy a 50/50 bar. The song I remember from that time, though, is one about singing in the sunshine. I took that song to heart. She was a gypsy, the woman in the song, and she stayed with people for one year and then took off after lots of laughter and love and singing and I thought that sounded like a damned good life.

When I hear that song now, and it is rare, I get teary. I think of Johnny and the way he would hit my mother with the rounded precision of a wrecking ball. The last time he did, my mother told him, after picking herself up from the grass, "If you do that again in front of her, you'll find a knife in your back." For years, most of my life, in fact, I thought she had meant me, that I would do this thing. I was five and my mother had just given me great power, all that she had left at the time, I had thought. I wish I had understood all that time that she was protecting me. So much comes down to perception. All directions are open and we take a multitude of phantom journeys. Perhaps that is the nature of journey. Mine, that day, took me down the road to a decision: I would be perfect, even if it killed me, because no one messes with a perfect person.

I was young.

Later that same day, after Johnny had gone into town and everyone could finally relax, my mother asked, "And what does Mesa want to be when she grows up" I shot back, "I want to be perfect, because I am not coming back here!" That cleared the room. Everyone left and headed for the kitchen to discuss my proclamation, amid laughter and sidelong glances in my direction. I walked outside, past the grinning dog and sat alone on the hill behind the house. Under an August, sky laced with stars, wishing stars, I waved my hands out in front of my face—creating a shower of little stars and mini-planets that trailed my fingers in the dark. This brought me joy, and best of all, loving companions. They sparkled and danced in the air around my head, each one singing its own note, together weaving a melody that I then danced to round and round in the grass. I believed in them, and more importantly, they believed in me, always.

Actively pursuing perfection was going to be a mighty weight on my shoulders and I would need real friends. True ones.

That was a very long time ago. And I am still hungry. My body, unfamiliar with emptiness, is filling with voices. And being here is beginning to piss me off in a big way. What am I supposed to do here? Lay in the sand. Run in the sand. Walk in the sand. Sand. For days. Starve and think about all of the crap in my Everything I have worked hard to forget...that's all there is to do.

I could dance again—I don't want to let this mood take hold. I knew being in the heat would get my personal crap moving. I could lie back and let it all come up to the surface, look at it and see where it wants to go. Sounds easy enough, but it's hard to be somewhere that has nothing to distract me from my mind. From my life, and how much I hate it. Nothing to pull my attention from how little I love myself. Nothing between myself and the echoes of people who loved me even less.

Echo: 1963

"Why don't you come in here, girls? Cartoons are on the TV and I have a bowl of candy. See? It's over there, right on the coffee table," he said with a wave of his hand. There was black under and around his fingernails, outlining each.

My friend and I were six years old. We lived next door, on either side of him. After we came in, he asked us to come in the bathroom with him. He wanted to check to see how much we had grown since the last time he had seen us out playing. My friend scooped up a handful of little candies from the bowl and stuck most of them in her mouth. She looked at him and then at me, just looking. We both followed him into the bathroom. I had taken some candy with me too as I walked behind my friend. He closed the door behind us. It wasn't a very big bathroom so we were all too close.

He smelled like bug spray and cigarettes when he pulled us close to him for a hug. Then, as he was hugging me, one arm around my shoulders, he reached his other hand slowly down the front of my pants. I looked at him and then at my friend who had pink drool on her chin. She was watching us. "Oh yes, that's good. You're a big girl. Everything is just fine. Thank-you." He smiled a wet smile and I noticed the sweat above his lip. When he took his hand out of my pants, I could still feel the impression of his fingers on me. I didn't like it. He then turned to my friend and I wanted to leave when he pulled her close.

Just to get outside. Play, anything, away from his smell and feel. My friend stood still while her checked her growth, dripping drool on her white tee shirt. Her hands were sticky with candy juice and pink fuzz. The smell of everything really started to bother me. I wanted to leave. "We have to go home. We're supposed to stay in the yard," I said.

"You two better go then. Don't tell anyone, now. Alright? This is our secret—here, take this candy with you, girls." We left when he opened the bathroom door and then closed himself back in. When we got to the front door, I looked back at the bathroom and still felt his hand in my pants, like I was carrying it around. I turned the knob and we went outside to play. We never talked about it and we never went back.

Okay, I don't see the point of bringing up all of that stuff again. What can I really do with it? I don't even know who he was, and even if I did, what good would it do to confront him, or others? How can I relieve myself of pain by dumping it on someone sicker than myself? So, what do I do with my anger? My sadness?

My whole life has felt like a long sadness. A big empty sad. And there is no one, only me, to take and do something with it. Something good, something helpful, something happy in the end. Maybe that is why God/dess brought me here. And there are no knights. We have to do it ourselves. I know this isn't news to anyone, maybe I'm just slower than the norm. And it isn't fair. It isn't fair that it was just left for me to work out. I didn't offer myself up. People touched me with their disease and left me to die slowly. Sometimes I think if I had a gun, I would turn it on myself. Who gives a damn.

I guess it is fortunate that God/dess had chosen to make me barren, knowing how useful deserts are to those who have nothing anyway. Maybe I will never leave. Maybe I carry her with me forever. Maybe I am the desert. Makes me feel a real kinship with the planet. Maybe that's what keeps us all from falling off--relationship.

What would I give a kid if I could create one? No boundaries--I don't know where I start or end. And dry, the water that runs through this desert is needed for my own survival. It evaporates the hot minute it touches the ground.

I wonder if this is the kind of crap Jesus had to go through in the desert--I don't know anything about his being violated as a child. I think that was saved for later.

Is this the devil, then?

Echo: 1962

"Mesa, come in here." A big bald man is calling me from the bathroom. He's my babysitter. I don't want to go. It's a small bathroom and he's very big. I walk over, taking my time. He shuts the door behind me, even though no one else is in the house.

"Come here. Hold this." He is talking quietly, but still scares me. "Do you like that, hmm? Rub it. Like this." Using my hand to hold himself, not looking at me, like I am not even there. My hands are burning up, but I am cold inside. The stars I hold within are shining so brightly, that he is blinded by the light. I know this because he cannot see me .

He must know I have stars inside. He must have seen them fall from my fingers. He is trying to take them, my stars, but I will not let them out. I stare hard at my hand, wrapped around him and will my fingers to stay closed. I hear the wind inside my head then just float away, knowing my fingers, my hands, will not betray me. I float away and do not look back. I have touched him privately with my magic, behind another closed door. A quiet miracle. I will be a saint someday. I will die a martyr. I will die.

Maybe I am already dead. They do not see me when I am there, shining so brilliantly.

Echo: 1965

I hear breathing, fast breathing. And something is very warm in my hand. I am waking up in the dark and my hand is draped over something smooth, something kind of hard, and there is a mouth on me. A tongue. I know who this is, kissing me between the legs while my mother sleeps in the next room, but it's dark and I cannot see anything. I can't move. I'm stuck. I am full awake in my body now and I want to fade back, back to the black of dream and stars. I want to throw up, the sound is making me sick.

Everything is too wet. It feels good. This is wrong. Maybe I'm drowning. I am dreaming. A new dream. I hate this. Hate my body, hate him. I'm afraid my mother will wake up and hate me too. If I didn't have a body he wouldn't be here with me doing this. I wouldn't be scared hot and wet and drowning. I would not be so awake. Too awake. I am not opening my eyes...there are stars in a black sky. I had stars on my birthday cake last week

and pink frosting and eight candles. There is too much wet. It
will put out the candles.

He came to me in the kitchen, set me on the counter, and I rolled
myself up in a ball and just rocked, under the dark window filling
with stars, stars, stars. I drew my fists up tight, so he wouldn't
see that they fell from my fingers all the time. So he would not
try to touch my magic. It was mine. I would not share it with him.
Not with anyone. I had already learned how to not talk with my
body, to hide deeply within.

I lay there in a ball, dreaming of one day being an artist. I would
paint a beautiful world with an immense sky, where my stars could
live free. There would be a full moon. I would be in this painting
too, alone on a desert island, in the middle of the largest sea,
under a magical twilit sky. The moonlight casting a thin sheet
over my curled body. And there I would stay, hanging on
someone's wall; someone who spent all they had to buy my vision.
And they would look at me forever, love me forever, want
me. And I would return those feelings, as long as I could hang
there on the wall, forever.

Echo: 1966

"You are a cunt. Say it," said my neighbor.

"Cunt," I repeated.

"Say, 'I am a cunt'," he pushed.

"I am a cunt," I said.

"Don't forget it," he said.

And then he took me in a locked room, full of magazines with pictures of big-breasted women. I stood behind him, there next to his chair, looking at the pages he pointed at. I hated these women for being so large and impossible to hide. And I hated him even though he was a friend of sorts. He was, more than anything else, the only company I had. So, we did what he wanted, for the most part. Until the first time I cried because it felt good and it swept through my body like a betrayal. He never touched me again after that.

I was nine then and later grew to have large breasts that I had already learned to hate. Because they reminded me of him-- his smell, his look, his movement, everything about him made me ashamed. And I knew I smelled the same because he had touched me. I had let him. Hatred smells, no matter where it is directed. Mine was carried within and so I had to smell within and was sure that everyone knew it. He always smelled of sex, never of love. I could never find beauty in the smell of sex after him.

I grew up longing for convents and monasteries and eventually, hermitage. I could not even be a part of a religious community or whole. I wanted to be alone. A nun, a monk, a hermit, and turn any sensual ardor into religious passion. So, I became a hermit. And I grew fat for a time and locked my door, living a cloistered life with the same deadness of spirit I saw and felt around me. Almost dead. Just nearly. A spark of hope never died. A small light stayed within, but I could not fan it into flame for the longest time.

Echo: 1971

"Mesa, yer a sheep and always will be, " laughed my stepfather.

Beneath my breath, quietly pushing it from where my breath is borne, "Yeah, fuck you."

I cannot do this anymore. I can't fall apart. I have nothing else. There is no one else. I have nothing at all, but a cat with no loyalty. I would just disappear if everything came unglued now. I would fall here in pieces on the sand, the wind blowing me around. The echoes shaking my bones, tossing them about; breaking them down into dust. Maybe I am lying here on centuries of women's bones.

These unkind voices, they just really love me boy. Their pale hands touch me, mouths touch me and I feel nothing but my bones breaking down. They call out for chorus, and images gather. I see cunts and penises and breasts and mouths and too many dead, starless hands. And I hear lies on the wind and it sickens me. I am pieces, blown apart and my voice is not loud enough to pull me together. I am not whole. And I hate those who wasted me and left me to throw myself away. And this hatred hurts more than anything else; smells like death, but it is alive, moving within me, hot, and there, at least, I can warm my disembodied hands.

The air has changed sentiment; she feels cold and I feel

abandoned. I don't understand why there are places like this, or why I came, as if the voices in my life were not already loud enough. Like they needed a bigger space to run amok and leave no witnesses. But there is a witness. There is supposed to be a witness. Where is God/dess?

Everything is giving way, spilling out, running off. I am just letting it go. I want to be left alone with just the simple point of "me" that is witnessing this death. Even broken apart, the pieces each contain the whole. Perhaps this is a loving process and the true nature of love sharp and clear—absolute, no matter where you draw the line. Purifying like fire, amplifying like crystal, or a blade that cuts away the cancer; it is healing. Love. Like the opposite of sympathy and stickiness--empathy, that is the brighter light; the higher octave to sentimentality—the music that usually oozes from the radio. True love will come through one song and set a fire, clearing a path through the rest. You can feel it. Love is powerful.

I want to be held with true love. Don't clog my pores; I cannot breathe when I am full up on syrup. That is how I feel now, burn me with the truth, but tomorrow, still alone, I may want to drown in sweet.

The moon is up. I can still hear faint voices as they scatter across the sand, like tumbleweed at the mercy of the wind. I feel for them. They didn't kill me. I am still here. Is conception like this? A point of awareness, spreading out, trying to fill the space it has been poured into? No wonder we stare at our hands when they pass before our newborn eyes—our virginity. Look at what we have become. The echoes speak to me in my own voice. My heart talking to my mind; my mind talking to my heart; my heart screaming at my body, blaming her for everything. It isn't fair, really, everyone in there just looking out for themselves.

I believe I can hear the earth talking to me, calling me to Silence. "Let them go..." she says, but I feel too low to the ground without the voices in there; afraid I will disappear entirely, so I scan the horizon, looking for anything going up. I am looking for green.

The wind is blowing through me and I think of harmonicas, midnights, and travelers in the dark. Separate ones. Spaces between all of us; spaces within ourselves. Movements in the dark I have known all of my life. I have been afraid of the dark as long as I can remember. I see, though not without mighty effort, that they have been a gift. A strange, unbeautiful gift, ragged and sharp; given unconsciously, accepted and kept over the years. A gift in ugly torn paper, carrying it around; yanking, tearing, pulling the paper a bit at a time until finally, the gift, the treasure, lay exposed, sitting there amid the ruins of its keeper. A mighty, precious thing...my Self.

And in this larger state, while I can feel this big, I hold myself in the dark, under a bright full moon and declare, "I am whole. I am indivisible and cannot be penetrated." And in this moment it is absolutely true.

I wasn't sure why I came here, but now I don't care. Behind my eyes, I fade into the sky and then come the stars. I am not afraid of the dark tonight. A miracle.

Day Two:

"Across the desert, grew a phantom. And there arose a great clamor—peal without bell; cry without throat; want without, the loudest of all.

Phantom, lover, I cast you myself."

Well yesterday was a lot of fun. Last night though, I had a wild dream about a sphinx moth. They have dust on their wings. Touch their wings and rob them of flight—so I've heard. I asked her, my moth, in the dream. She smiled, so small, so immense. She told me, "No, this is one of many stories. There are many in this world because the stories create spaces between each other; caves. Look between the stories and you will see the caves. They contain Truth. Touch my wings. I come from the caves. I live in the dark looking for the light. When I find it, I am consumed by it. Touch me."

I had to lean up close, and she pulled me in, took me under her wing. "You have confused me with butterfly. I do not change. I am change. Look again for the cave. Here is a secret: slip your eye across all the stories, quickly, and you will notice patterns; waves of energy moving. Swells and shallows. Look and listen,

listen to the rhythm. Once you are familiar with the pattern, you will know where to find the break."

I did not understand a thing she was saying. These moths are famous for being cryptic, after all. You have to really want to understand, I think, and I did want to. I'm just not the swiftest person on the planet. Anyway, I was dusted by a creature of the caves, and moved to fly, so I will be free at night. So she said, in this dream.

You know, in a space this immense, here in the desert, where I occupy so little, the odds of my coming face to face with myself border on the miraculous. I am looking for that miracle. Although I am not looking for anyone to part the sea--It's been done.

It's nearly dawn and we, she and I, twin deserts, are waiting for the light. Predawn always brings big ideas. The things I try to drown out with coffee, mostly because I don't know what to do with big ideas. Here I am before the light, needing to voice and all of the familiar ones have run off across the desert. I'd sure like to read the desert notes of Jesus. When all of his human voices ran off across the sand, he was left with God and Satan. At least it was clear. I seem to just be left. I guess I am not a messiah.

iiiii...want to know who I am. What is my treasure? What do I
have to offer? And if I find it will I give it? I want to be like
Christ, or Buddha. Any of the giants. I want to be Divine.
That's the thing. I am stuck between the world and God/dess.
I want to let go completely, but I don't know how. I'm lying.
I never let go completely, because I don't want to, completely.

God/dess spoke a word and everything sprang into being.
The world. Then we learned to voice, and we, too, created
worlds. So words, sound, can create worlds and like a wine glass
at the mercy of a sustained high note, worlds can be destroyed
with opposite intent. And here we all are, walking around;
creators, destroyers, unaware of the art or rubble in our wake.
And unmindful of our own voice--our own particular sound, like
animals, within the tangle of so many.

But the voices do not walk. They limp. While they have been trying to run around inside of me, their awkward movements, their tendency to join together on one side, have thrown me off-center and forced me to walk with an emotional limp. Until I can distinguish between the truth of me, my own voice, and illusion, I will cast and list to one side. I cannot walk upright until I am whole.

Things look really different from the ground up. If you put your eye right up to something, it looks much bigger than it is because it is all you can see. It takes up your entire eye.

I smell hot dogs. I love hot dogs. I don't think I really want one. It just floated up to me, presenting itself as some kind of possibility. Aromas, voices, things you cannot see or touch, but treat as if they had a body you could get involved with. Memory is like that. And we plant new seeds in our memories every time we call them up or they drop in, because something new is there every time. Something different took root and changed the landscape when it parted the soil.

Memory is full of unexplored possibilities. It can grow the aroma of a street corner hot dog right here between a white hot sky and a table of desert. And the aroma of a hot dog takes me somewhere else , where there were no hot dogs that I remember.

Age 16
1973

Of course, I couldn't be alone and save some dignity; I was with two friends. It was my 16th birthday and I was along for one of those boring rides through town that every teenager in Yamhill repeated a good fifty times a day. It never took very long, Yamhill being but a three-blink town, so it could easily have been more than fifty. We were smoking pot.

I'm there in the car when the weirdest thing starts happening to me. I feel an invisible skin grow around me like a giant egg, about 8-12 inches out from my body. I couldn't see it, but I felt it growing like it was really there.

I was terrified; this wasn't a normal thing. My friends thought I'd really lost it and I would have too, if I weren't so focused on the thing happening to me. I asked them to pull it off of me and they were good sports about it. It gave them something to do and then later talk about to every living soul in town. It didn't help anyway. Oh well. Happy birthday.

I don't know why, but I thought maybe if I ate something I would somehow be cured or freed—I have carried this idea of miracle cure with me all through life and have yet to find any evidence to support it, but I don't care. So, I had my friends drive me to the 7-11 down the street and I bought a candy bar. It didn't help. Now I was trapped inside this skin, or whatever it was, with a sugar high. I went home.

I went to bed early, after making a number of promises to God for the return of my sanity and boring reality. Sanity might be as exciting as a bowl of cold oatmeal, but I have seen one of the alternatives, and I can learn to like cold oatmeal.

I slept for about eighteen hours, hoping the whole thing would wear off, or better yet, be some kind of dream. When I woke up after, something was different; everything was different, in some way. The world looked a bit unreal. Nothing bizarre--no cars floating upside down outside the window--just a general sketchiness to everything, like someone had taken a pencil and traced over everything. A drawing in progress or an idea not fully developed. It was weird and I did not like it at all.

It got worse.

I looked away from the window and there on the floor, in the corner, over my closet, sat a woman who looked a lot like me, only better. And older. Maybe thirty. She was kind of sketchy too. Not quite solid. Not a ghost, but a person with a lot of light leaking from the seams. The woman looked strange, but not in a bad way.

"Who are you?" I asked her.

"Hi Mesa. I'm Mega," she answered, smiled and got up, walked over to the bed.

"Mega? That's a weird name. Are you a friend of my mom's?"

"No, actually, I am a friend of yours. I've known you from the beginning." She was now standing next to the bed, looking down at me.

"The beginning? You mean since I was born?" She really didn't have to stand so close. I didn't even know her. It was bugging me.

"Well, maybe it would be easier to grasp if I just said 'I am you, but more'." With this, she sat down on the end of the bed. Okay. I decided to go back to sleep because this must have been a dream and sleep was my defense against anything strange invading my life.

"I'm going to sleep now...nice meeting you, really. Could you say hi to my mom on your way out?" I was pointing at the door, which was pretty rude for me, but jeez, really, why was all of this stuff happening to me? I didn't do drugs. Nothing serious. I could never get my hands on anything...so what...what was all of this?

"Look Mesa, I know this is hard to follow...I also know you have had a rough couple of days."

"How did you know that? Oh right, I forgot...you ARE me. Of course you would know." I started crying and felt like a wimp, but this woman, Mega, looked like she might care a little that I had lost my grip on reality and I liked her for that, even if I had made her up.

"Mesa, it's okay, really. Just relax. I didn't mean to scare you. It does sound a bit weird, I guess. I just want you to know that you are okay, and what you are and have been experiencing is not 'real'. Not entirely. When I say I am you, I mean that I am the real you, not the one that you believe yourself to be. Okay," she laughed, "these things have a tendency to sound hokey and cryptic..."

"You're an angel?" I had a dim understanding of what that might be, having watched a lot of movies about angels.

"Well, not your understanding of 'angel', no."

"A psychic? Or a spirit guide or something like that?" I asked.

"No. I am you. Your future. I was concerned about you, so I came in person to talk. Well, you are my person...let's just say I decided to drop in as a visual aid, because you don't listen much unless there is a body attached—a different one. Language is a pain. Let me put it this way. We could say that God/dess is Creativity and the Artist...and I am an artist and a creation. You are my idea and that idea is evolving, which in turn teaches me. You are also a tool for the expression of ideas, in addition to yourself, which makes you an artist and a creation as well. I am just closer to the creativity. And you created me."

"What?" My mouth was hanging open. I didn't think people really did that in moments of stupidity, but it's true. We do. "Do I need to know this stuff? I mean, I don't know what you are talking about."

"No, not now, not really. Will you just accept my presence and do what I ask?" She was serious.

"That depends. What are you going to ask me to do?" I had a right to ask, for crying out loud.

"All that's being asked of you is that you be the best artist you are capable of being. And the best artists knowingly embody Creativity. You cannot separate them from Art," she answered.

"I don't get it. How do you embody creativity?" I asked.

"If you realize that you and your life, that life itself—that is shared by everyone, are works in progress. That every moment there is potential for complete transformation, for the good, you can alter yourself and your life. If lots of people, enough, change their minds about life, everything would change in that instant. Humanity is approaching this crossroad now."

"So, you said I didn't really need to understand this stuff—right? As long as I let you boss me around?"

She just looked at me for a moment, a long one, and I felt a wave of idiocy pass through my brain, quickly. I just did not get it. And I wanted to take a bath.

"Guru, swami, prophet, healer, used-car salesperson, taco vendor, apple, fly, or purebred cat—they're all the same. Know what I mean? Everything, everything is an idea and then a creation. Understand?" She seemed to expect me to answer.

I was sitting on the edge of the tub by now, trying to get just the right temperature of scald and she was across from me, sitting on the wooden lid of the toilet. The sun was hot coming through the window, the light bright between us. I looked at her to see if she was kidding, but she didn't smile.

"No, Mega, I don't know what you mean. Not at all. I don't understand any of this. I don't know really who or what you are, why you are here or what is going on. I don't get any of it. Did I do something wrong? I feel like I'm being punished for something. What I really want is to take a bath and float off somewhere...can I talk to you later?"

She looked at me for a long time, which made me really self-conscious, like undressing in front of my mother, and forget that. I did not understand. Period. Why me? I had not asked for this, had not done anything really wrong that I could remember. I never killed insects, well, unless it was them or me. I couldn't even leave food in the bottom of the package it came in because I didn't want a stray macaroni or whatever to feel like it was left behind for somehow not measuring up. The more I thought on that, the clearer it became that I was truly pathetic. No wonder this was happening to me. I had lost it a long time ago and I was the only one who didn't seem to know.

"Mesa, you haven't done anything wrong. Nothing out of the ordinary. Okay? You need to see how wonderful you really are. It is essential to your future, your destiny. I know you don't understand now, but trust me. In the future you will look back at this episode as a blessing. And believe it or not, you're going to be deeply grateful. As for now, this may have been a bit premature. You may not be ready."

"No. Probably not. For what?" It sounded like she might be going to leave. I could at least listen to what she had to say. She sighed. "Ready to understand. I'm not sure...maybe I was wrong about you."

Okay. There are two things I know about myself: one is that I almost always feel like a zero. I have a hard time feeling good about myself or anything else for more than half an hour at a time, tops. I cannot help it. I try. I really do. Mostly, I don't know why I was ever put on the planet or why anything is the way it is. And two: I hate it when someone else feels the same way about me. It pisses me off. Then I have to somehow prove that I am superhuman because just being normal isn't good enough anymore. I have to be great or nothing at all.

I've done some pretty amazing stuff just to show people how common I really am. I believe it too, for about half an hour. And now, Mega, a woman I didn't even know, was telling me that maybe I didn't measure up.

"Wrong about me? Wrong about me how?" I asked.

She wouldn't look at me. She just sat there on the toilet lid, picking invisible lint off of her jacket. A nice jacket—charcoal gray. With jeans and black boots. I mention this only because she must have spent a good five minutes brushing off her boots, straightening her jeans and picking at her jacket before saying, "Well, I just thought that you were...a little...braver." She finally looked at me, then sighed and folded her hands. A few moments passed.

She stood up and reached out to shake my hand. "We will meet again, under better circumstances. You know, when you are ready to take some risks."

"Braver? I'm not...I..."

"What?" She looked genuinely confused.

"I am...I can...be brave."

"Oh?" her sincerity was pretty insulting.

"You could at least tell me what all of this is about. You can't expect a person to just jump up and volunteer for something they know nothing about. It's just weird. I mean, would you? I'm not an idiot or a coward, if that's what you think." I glanced up at her to see if that was, in fact, what she thought. I don't know why I cared, but I did. Five minutes before I had just wanted her to leave; disappear. Now, I wanted her to know I was, I don't know, worthy of her attention or something. I'm not sure what I thought. I just didn't want her to leave yet. Not thinking I was a coward.

She sat back down on the toilet, smiled. "Here's an idea: you can do whatever you want, be who you want to be, even if someone else thinks differently. Idea #2: everyone is worthy of another's attention, and three—you are brave. You're still on the planet. That takes tremendous courage."

"You weren't really going to leave, were you? I was sorry I had wimped out so fast.

"No, but you cut it pretty close. I was running out of things to do with my clothes and was about to start on the toilet paper, but I didn't want you to think I was weird or anything," she smiled.

"I've never met anyone, you know, anyone real, who enjoys themself as much as you do." I said.

"I enjoy humor. It's a gift. And ...I am real. More real than you but we'll discuss that some other time. I need to take off," she smiled and her body started to glow, fading into the air. "I wanted to introduce myself, so you'd know you aren't alone—to help you through some things, and to encourage you to keep growing. I am waiting for you out there."

Although I didn't see Mega for years after this meeting, it was the beginning of my formal apprenticeship with her: my higher expression. My future, because somewhere I made the decision to keep growing. I know it seems weird, like I just made it up or something, but it's true, and she is real. She was real then and is now, and she came to me to help get me down the road to where she'd patiently been waiting from the beginning. She was real and I was not. Not absolutely.

And I could have lied...could have said that I went deep into the Amazon Jungle in South America, to apprentice with a shaman, but really, the trees are thinning there, so it isn't a true jungle anymore. Or all the way to Tibet, but the Dalai Lama isn't there, or the Mexican desert, but the truth is, I began my apprenticeship at home, in hot water. Exploring the vast potential of personhood—stretching the boundaries of my mind beyond the bathroom walls, in search of ...perfection. Divinity, God/dess.

Of course, at the time, I had no idea I was doing this. I never know anything really, when it's happening. Anyway, 1973 was a long time ago. Now I am here in a desert. Forsaken...the sun has moved, so I guess time has too. Shadow is moving over sand, dividing me. It cannot be more than five in the afternoon. I had forgotten about Mega. I've forgotten a lot of things. You would expect to forget the things that pierce you—to bury them somewhere, but I have put away even the things that can shield me from attack. Maybe I need to be pierced. Maybe healing one's wounds creates a wholeness altogether better than that of virginity. Maybe that is what one must think when one has no choice. I'm not a kid anymore. I am a woman, but unclaimed until now. By myself, I mean. And I want that woman that I am, with all the love, passion, and dream that I can call up.

Day Three:

Apprenticeship

Very early morning, the sky is not fully awake--foggy. It's cold, but last night's dream was warm.

Dream:

In the moonlight, from my bed, I saw her pacing back and forth, maybe twenty feet away on a rise above me. I was lying there under an August sky of wishing stars that cast their webs across the heavens. The water, a skinny skein of river, below, down an embankment directly behind my head, reflected the tracery above.

And just ahead, pulled to and fro; attention drawn to a point and moving gracefully in space; a visual chant, was the Trickster—Coyote. According to Native American stories, she is sacred, but unpredictable and wise in spite of herself. I had come here unaware, to her territory. I've heard that she likes fools and I probably had that occupation stamped all over my person.

I called to her, "Excuse me... I hope I am not in your way? I see that I am between you and the water. I can leave if you want, or I could stay and you could join me." I didn't feel like moving, even if it was appropriate, and hoped she did not sense my lack of enthusiasm for gracious gesture.

She laughed, longer than necessary, I think, walked slowly down the embankment for a drink, pulling several stars from the surface of the water as she drank. Then she turned to look at me. Coming back up the small steep hill, she stood facing me. I was sitting up now, amused by her total disregard for social nicety— she was enjoying making me uncomfortable and I was enjoying her enjoyment of herself. I hadn't seen this much, enough, in people. It was refreshing.

She laid down, about three feet away and looked up at the sky. She sighed, like the last breath of a steam engine. Well, okay, not quite that dramatic, but enough to draw pity if one were so inclined. I didn't quite trust her and I felt guilty about that, being human and easily distracted from the important things, so I wasn't leaning in her direction at all. "You, (sigh) are so fortunate." She looked at me when she said this, with such sincerity, and sadness, that I almost scooped her up to rock in my arms.

"Fortunate? What do you mean? I mean, iknowihavealottobethankfulfor...but what exactly do you mean?" I tried not to look like I desperately wanted her answer, which I did, so tried putting a mildly amused and somewhat curious expression out there on my face (coyotes make me really self-conscious).

"You have a great love coming your way...soon. Very soon." She said, raising her paws heavenward.

I chuckled, "I don't think so, no offense. I just don't think I have a great love scenario in my life. Not that I'd object if it were to come my way, but I don't see it happening, really. I've pretty much resigned myself to being alone for the rest of my life, working for God/dess." I sighed, like the last breath of a steam engine.

She covered her mouth with both paws and I saw out of the corner of my eye that her chest was heaving. I knew it, she was laughing. I tried not to let on that I had noticed, started brushing sand off my legs and things like that, and then she really could not contain herself. She spluttered laughter in the direction of the water and took a deep breath before turning back to me. I was above all of this, believe me. I just rubbed my eye with my sandy hand, tried to smile. I got enough humiliation out in the world, I wasn't about to get all upset with a coyote I didn't even know.

"I'm sorry Mesa. Don't be offended. I am just so filled with joy…because you are very mistaken about this love. I'm telling you that the greatest love of your life, your soul-mate, if you like, is on the way, soon. Trust me." She was good.

"Well, it's very generous of you to share this with me, Coyote. Thank-you. Is there anything I can do for you, to repay your generosity?" I asked.

"Just remember who told you when this love comes to pass. That will be reward enough. I wish you well and goodnight, for now." With that, she ran off into the sagebrush across the way, into the dark.

How kind she had been--her sincerity so touching. Still, Coyote.

It came to pass. Coyote was right. A great love did come into my life. I wasn't looking for it, being busily dissatisfied with myself and not seeing far beyond the dream of my future perfection—the answer to all of my problems. The Universe however, the unseen things, the loving movements of air and sound and aroma, all coalesced to make a specter of love, that called to me in regular conversation, "Hey, Mesa."

It was a woman.

In the very early morning, in the same spot as Coyote from last night's dream, was Mega. "Hey Mesa..." she called again. Very pale stars danced around her head.

"Did you bring coffee?" I asked.

She laughed. "Ah, I see you're right up against it. Guess I'll go before it gets ugly."

"Right up against what?" I asked, starting to feel cranky from no infusion of caffeine.

"Wilderness. Don't worry about your surroundings. You've found what you're looking for," she smiled and stayed out of reach.

"What was I looking for? I wasn't looking for anything. Some stupid dream told me to come here. I wasn't looking to freeze, roast, starve, and smell."

"Hmmm...I'm going now. I just wanted to say hi and remind you that you did ask for this. See you soon." She left, walking back in the direction from which she had just come.

Then Mega's voice danced in space, right by my left ear.

"Wilderness is, beyond a pathless region, a path unto itself. We are all on it, though unaware."

I turned in the direction I believed her voice to be coming from and felt the air move in a spiral, like a baby wind funnel. "You can come back. I won't be awful to you. It's actually, really great that you came. I haven't talked to anyone, well, no one human. It's too quiet and you must have come for a reason—right? Did you bring coffee? You do know, don't you, that it's considered good manners to bring a gift when you come to visit someone? Like, oh...coffee, or even chocolate. Anything."

The space by my ear, where a moment ago there had been a spiral of air, where Mega's voice moved over the sand, shimmered and Mega appeared whole, right there, so close that her knee bumped hard up against my ear.

"Ow!" I said.

"Oh, sorry." she said.

"Coffee?" I smiled, hoping.

"Sorry, just me," she raised her empty hands, "but you know, here is a thought for you. If you find something in your mouth a lot of the time—food, coffee, cigarettes, fingernails, whatever, it is only this: keeping in close contact with your mouth, just to remember that you have the means to voice. Find your voice, say what you have to say and your mouth will be less interesting to you."

"Thanks, really profound...and I caught it without benefit of caffeine."

"It's maddening, isn't it?" she asked.

"What? No coffee?" I asked, feeling slightly drugged; my tongue starting to feel kind of hairy and overbig.

"Here, have some water." She handed me a plastic jug with warm water.

"Ugh. It always tastes like plastic in those jugs. I hate that. And it's warm."

"Drink some water. Boy, you're a lot of fun today. I guess I could be more sympathetic. It's hard letting go of addictions."

"Hey Mega, excuse me, but I hardly do anything anymore. Coffee is little league stuff. It isn't like I am downing a quart of whiskey a day or gambling away my wealth," which made me laugh, because wealth and I had yet to meet.

"The more you release, the clearer your mind, body, and emotions become. Then you can begin to notice the strong effect other things have actually been having on you. You released cigarettes and sugar, so you are not getting hit by a truck on a regular basis, but you are still walking against traffic, getting knocked around by VW's.

"So, what happens when I don't have any of those things in my body? Then do I get to rest? Rest and be bored because there is no longer anything fun to do. Or is there something else beyond them that I then have to get rid of?" Images of desert after desert stretched before my inner eye. It was depressing.

"You heal as well as you are able then help others to do the same. Healing isn't always, well, it isn't pleasant, but once you get through it, you'll be a new woman. I promise."

"How long? My tolerance is not long or high." I asked. "As long as it takes. The world is big. The people are many. Lamentations of a bodhisattva..."she laughed, drawing circles in the sand between us.

"What's a bodhisattva?"

"A person who promises to wait to enter enlightenment after everyone else has reached it," she answered.

"Wait a minute. Are you talking about me? I didn't promise anything of the kind. What is the point of trying to better myself if I have to wait for others who don't care about bettering themselves, before I reach enlightenment?"

"Well," she answered, "don't wait. Help others while you help yourself. Everyone gets there sooner."

"You mean, and this is a depressing thought, I go to all of this trouble, trying to heal and be myself and everything, and then I don't even get to hang out and enjoy my perfection? I just have to jump right back into the muck with everyone else?"

"Perfection? Perfection is an interesting idea," she smiled, "but how about this...let's talk about near-perfection. It will give you more hope."

"I see. How about you just tell me why you' rehere," I pouted.

"Don't be so easily discouraged, Mesa. You give yourself a tall order like perfection, you have to be pretty tall. You really have to stretch. It isn't about you alone, though. Selflessness is the keynote of perfection. Are you ready to totally surrender your whole self, your way of life, and identity, on behalf of others, to a higher purpose?" she asked.

She looked compassionate as she asked me that question-- another expression I do not enjoy receiving from others.

"Sacrifice does not come easily to your nature, if you don't mind my noticing," she continued.

"Actually, yes, I do mind."

"Well, okay. Aside from all that, how are you feeling?"

"Feeling? Right now I feel depressed. Like, if I can't reach perfection, if I can't be some great spiritual leader or something, what do I do with myself? I mean, I thought I had been called apart for some special purpose, you know? I was inspired and everything. Now I have nothing to look forward to. I'll be the same nobody I was before. And I feel spent. Like I'm empty or flat. The last couple of days...I feel like I've been tricked or betrayed. You know? I don't understand why my life has to be like...like what it is...and what it isn't, when I see the lives of others being so wonderful and exciting or anything other than the way mine is. I just feel tired. Really tired. Mostly, I'm tired of never understanding anything. I think I'd really like to be alone right now, if you don't mind."

"Mesa…" she moved over and touched my face, which made me cry.

"Look, don't do anything meaningful, or out of the ordinary. I cry for no reason at all the last couple of days."

"Mesa, I want you to know, you have been very brave. Don't be so quick to put a period on things. Things are usually different than we believe them to be. You haven't been singled out by the Universe for despair, no matter how it appears to you. So, don't give up, stay open. The desert seems harsh and lonely but the kindest spirit lives here. Stay open. If you don't I won't see you again. And know that you will not be the same woman when you leave here. Be kind to yourself."

I was crying like a baby left out in an alley. The world seemed heartless. My existence would pass into the air like a single outbreath of a racing sprinter. This woman then cradled me like a Great Mother, which made me feel really self-conscious for a moment, until I remembered she was really me, and if I couldn't let go in my own arms, I could never hold anyone else or even be honestly in the arms of another. I would never really hold anyone. So I just relaxed and cried. After what seemed an eternity, tears dried on my face, the skin was tight and my eyes felt pushed up all out of their sockets, like trying to escape a flood.

"Why does crying have to destroy your face when it feels so good? There's a price on everything, for crying out loud," I said, wiping my face.

"Your face isn't destroyed. You look lovely and real. Don't carry the world with you in private," she said.

"Oh, right...what? Leave it back where I got it? How do you not take it with you everywhere? I don't know how to let go of the world, and I would love to, now that I've had all this time to think about what it's given me." I started crying all over again. I knew she was going to bring up something about self-pity, because I was enjoying my dive out into the middle of it, but she did not. She just wiped my face and said nothing.

Then, "I am here, as I said, to say hi and...after a couple of days with no food or drug, I think you are clear enough to do some focused work."

"Mega, I think you're being a little dramatic about the drug thing. I said I haven't exactly been horizontal in an opium den, remember?"

"Now, that really is an interesting image. See how creative minds get when the edges are not dulled?"

She stretched out in the sand, put her arms under her head, crossing her legs at the ankles. "Do you feel like working?" she asked.

"Working? Do I have to move?" I lay back in the sand.

"Not your body, but you do have to pay attention. I want to work on your visualization. All of that imagination needs to get a little less self-centered and more productive, if you know what I mean."

"Are you talking about my fantasies? Is there something wrong with imagining things that I like or want if it feels good?"

"No, but you could use some of your creativity in service to others," she said. A huge obnoxious fly kept buzzing around my head. I didn't think flies lived in the desert and I pondered this for a moment. I read somewhere that flies are just manifestations of all our trash thoughts. Of course, some human would think of that. God/dess knows that flies couldn't have some kind of fly-specific reason for being here.

Then I thought about killing it. I could. I was bigger. Not long ago, maybe a few days, I happily would have murdered the fly, but something new was being born in me, I guess—compassion, maybe, for the other pathetic creatures of the world. I was probably as much a product of my own trash thoughts as the fly, so why not have mercy? The favor might be returned one day when a thing bigger than myself was pondering my annoying existence in their world. I left the fly alone and it flew away.

"Mesa."

"What? Oh, sorry. Yes, I see your point. I've never done that though, you know, shared my visions with others or used them or whatever. You mean help others somehow?"

"Yes, it's a tool to be used, but not just for yourself. It's a gift and a gift is a thing of movement, to be shared, not hoarded. You have practiced enough imagining for your own pleasure, now it is time to learn how to give it in service."

"Jeez, have you been reading my mind all this time? I hate that. Am I supposed to feel guilty now? I feel guilty. I haven't been trying to hog it or anything. I never thought that there might be a shortage of imagination in the world or people starving for it."

She looked at me long enough to make me uncomfortable. "Well, there are. You have people starving for food before they can even tend to their dreams and pleasure. And then, most people don't even know the imagination's power as a tool. It changes everything for the good, when used correctly—for others and not the self, alone. In service, it is Divine Expression. It moves mountains, or creates them. You'll see." She poked me hard between the eyes.

"Ow!" I said, rubbing my forehead, and then this vision started forming. I heard music.

Vision

A black and white film with a kind close-up with soft lighting, of my blemish-free face fills the frame. My skin is moist and lips are parted. Then the camera moves back and a man's shirt on my body, is unbuttoned far enough to reveal an ample breast. Music seems to grow from the very ground I stand on. As the camera slowly backs away, revealing my surroundings—an endless panorama of cacti. A mountain rises behind me. I lift my right arm in slow motion, flipping back long locks of hair from across my face. I start walking toward the camera, gracefully, of course, with long strides of my perfectly curved, not too muscular, clean-shaven legs. I am pouting slightly, and the wind, always this cooperative, is keeping my hair back from my face. The background music swells, builds in pitch, the beat becoming harder.

Then I trip and fall on a really hairy cactus to my right and scream. This snaps me right out of this vision. I open my eyes, feeling kind of light, like a weight had been lifted. Mega is laughing her head off. "That stuff can really trip you up, can't it? It's not all your creation, but you've bought it. Call it 'eroticastigmatism'. There's nothing to it, just distortion, so let it go. You need to release your addiction to appearances, and your focus on yourself as the center of the Universe. Try again." Putting my hand up to my forehead so she wouldn't poke me again, I closed my eyes.

(Note:

I have bought into this whole image thing and it has messed up my perception of priority. I cannot love who I am if I am told, and believe, that who I am is not what I should be because something or someone else is worthy of love and adoration and I am not because I am not that or her or she or whatever. Anyway, to love me, I have to see and accept the truth of who I am and find comfort in knowing that this is true for everyone else too. We can be unsure and miserable together.)

Vision

I am dressed like John Wayne as a cowboy, standing in the middle of a lot of dust and tumbleweed, talking to a minister.

"This town is very churchified, Padre." I say, chewing on a dead stogie, which tastes nasty and is the reason I am scowling.

"That's right, Miss. A God-fearing town, you can rest assured," he beamed.

"That's what I was afraid of, Padre."

"Why, I don't think I take your meaning. And mind you, I don't think that is any way for a lady to talk. Why aren't you at home anyway? Have you no family to care for?" he asked with a scowl of his own. No stogie.

"Yes, Padre, I do have a family to care for. Just a moment. Would you wait here?" I felt a speech rising within me.

(Soliloquy: I turn and step up to an unseen audience.)

"Okay folks. I see people coming out of the churches, dressed nicely, getting into fancy carriages, walking right by the woman in the doorway holding three dirty children; the man stumbling from the saloon and falling into the street; the girls in short leather skirts, high heels and painted faces; the young boys in too tight pants, with no expression, leaning against the wall, watching every passing horse and rider.

And I have to ask myself, knowing there is only that—the search for Truth; who are the good guys and who are the bad? And...if this is MY vision, do I use it to quietly decorate my private life, or do I take this tool, this new weapon, stick it in my holster and ride forth to help conquer the enemies, if I can figure out who they are?"

I turned back to the minister.

"Thanks, Padre, for waiting," I said.

"Woman, I was listening to that blasphemy, and people in these parts don't take kindly to strangers coming into to town, stirring up trouble or to women who don't know their place. Does your husband know where you are?"

"I ride alone, Padre. And excuse me, yes, I do have work to do. Good day to you," tipping my hat, I spat out the stogie.

(End of vision)

Smiling as the vision fades, I open my eyes, "I go forth, to dream, to ponder, or clean up this world...that was pretty good, don't you think? I was thinking of others." I looked over at Mega.

"Where did you learn to swagger and talk like John Wayne?" she asked.

"Movies, of course. Pretty good, right?"

"Did you ride off into the sunset?" she asked.

"Oh, I didn't notice...I don't think I had a horse...do you want me to go back and see?" I closed my eyes.

She poked me in the forehead again.

"Ow! Why do you keep doing that?" I asked.

"You are still focused on you. You want to be a hero? Or do you really want to help others? Try again and let yourself get quiet. Get below all of the noise and goings-on. See what is there."

"Okay," I closed my eyes. "There is nothing wrong with being heroic...how is anything going to get done if no one's heroic?" I mumbled.

(Note:

This one is hard for me because being a hero, being needed— not just by one person, but by the whole world, is one of my favorite fantasies. Obviously, doing something heroic is harder. Saving people is pretty stressful and often dangerous and you really have to be good about timing your appearance on the scene. The hardest, though, is the heroic stuff no one else ever knows about--you know, like really continuing to love someone who's right up in your face, hating you for all they are worth. That is pretty brave and amazing and what credit do you get? You might get killed or something--great payoff, but it is a major act of heroism. Loving is a major act of heroism, because so much is stacked against it actually happening.

"Okay, we'll try again," I said.

Vision

Another black and white movie—this time with a deserted street corner, about eleven o'clock at night. A streetlamp and me, the only things standing there. It's foggy, making everything look dreamlike. Off in the distance, maybe a block away, someone is playing music loud enough for it to drift down the street to me and this light, alone on the corner.

It is an old song, from the forties, I think. I feel like dancing, but I'm alone. I'm in the mood for romance, but I have no partner. So, I just start dancing, sometimes with the streetlight, sometimes just off and by myself. I have all the makings of something I want, that I would share with someone else, but I have to give it to myself alone. I do a great soft shoe, there on the moist sidewalk. It sounds like a shoe on a sandy board, and I am sliding around like I really know what I am doing. It doesn't matter that I don't. The dance is for me—a gift to my own body. (End of vision)

"I liked that, but still, you need to expand your focus," Mega squinted over at me. "Why can't you take yourself out of your vision?"

"You know, Mega, I don't feel like I get so awfully much that it is some kind of crime to give it to myself. If no one else is giving it, why shouldn't I give it to me, if I need it?"

"You are absolutely right. I want you to understand something, though. Others are giving it—just in many forms. And you truthfully need and want to be alone right now because you are healing. You do need to love yourself, a great deal. The Universe is not trying to withhold any good stuff from you, so don't let it hurt your feelings when you find yourself alone. It won't be that way forever. You need time with yourself right now, to love yourself into wholeness. However, when you give only to you, you gain, but others gain only indirectly—secondhand. When you give to others first, everyone gains and you get so much, directly. And if you are able to give first, and I mean give without hope of getting something, anything, in return, it will be an indication that you are healing, because whole persons live lives of gift." She looked at me, seeing if I understood.

"Okay...living a life of gift...let's try again." I closed my eyes.

(Note:

A great love story is a great love story, regardless of the audience. If there is no one else around but your body, give it to yourself, this dance. We emotionally abuse our bodies without even noticing. They deserve some good stuff too. We usually don't see it that we're getting it from all directions anyway—love, I mean. "Relationship is a huge word, but we make it very small—fitting only two people in one situation.")

Vision

I'm at a packed nightclub, waiting around for someone to ask me to the floor and that gets boring after awhile, so I just go by myself, which, really, is what I wanted anyway. I am dancing and feeling pretty good, when my body starts feeling like it wants to go in circles, you know, like you do when you're a kid. It is like the whirling dervish thing the Sufis do, although I think they have a lot of spirit involved with their dance. I just felt kind of moved to do it, so I did.

After a few minutes, I notice that I have more room to move in, I'm not hitting people anymore, so I open my eyes. Everyone, I mean everyone, in staring at me. They have formed a circle around me, in fact. I stop whirling around, get kind of nauseous for a moment, and ask them what the problem is. They just look at me like I have something disgusting on or about my person and start dancing again. I decide I do not need this, and leave.

I walk about a mile out to the desert, and I feel this tremendous
urge to dance in circle again. So, I do. I do for about fifteen
minutes, feeling the difference in my sense of balance, meaning I
am not swaying like a top that's gonna fall over any minute. All
of a sudden, I glance down and notice there is something like
rose-colored fog growing up around my legs and feet, spiraling
around me. It's weird. And then I look at my outstretched
hands, swinging out in space, which was not an easy thing to do
without feeling queasy.

Colors seem to be draining from my surroundings and being
sucked up into my hands. Soon, the black and white of
everything follows the color, and disappears into the ends of my
fingers. There is nothing outside of myself— not black or white,
not color, just not anything. My ability to distinguish between
things also seems to have disappeared with them.

It was kind of exciting. I wondered if I started dancing in the
opposite direction, if it would all come back out again.

And, could I change it somehow? Could I throw it out
differently than I took it in? I tried it. I was swinging round and
round, flinging my hands out at my sides, as if giving some might
gift to the world. I tried to alter my hand movement, make it
different than when I took stuff in. And I was swinging so fast
that I must have appeared to be one big blur of outstretched
hand, moving in space.

Anyway, it happened. I thought of sending the world back out in a brighter, lighter form; I threw out all of the love and joy and curiosity I could find within, and sent these things out through my fingers to land where they may. My fingers danced and threaded through the air. I was a tornado with all but its eye being cast from itself.

And the world began to take form. It was radiant and raised the hair on my arms, it was so alive. Here was a place I would gladly stay...this desert, my desert, was singing and shimmering around me.

(End of vision)

"Very good. See? You don't have to dig very deep to find the treasure." She mussed my hair.

I was on a roll. Feeling very generous, like I could just create paradise for everyone right now and hand it over with all of the love I could possibly muster.

(Note:

When we learn to love our own bodies—even if everything around that we see and hear says we are wrong to do so—then we can expand on this. It's okay to bump into people while you dance your dance. If you keep practicing, you'll either discover some innate grace, or people will learn to get out of your way. And the longer you can manage to stay on your feet while you dance circles around everyone, the more familiar you will become with balance. If you balance, everything in relation to you is altered as well. Balancing the self sets a bunch of other stuff in motion too. Not bad for a dance.)

"And now, you need to see what stands in the way of your moving into the woman you really are—which is me, by the way. It must be released, this obstacle," said Mega. I closed my eyes.

Vision

There is an archway between here, where I am standing, waiting, and there, where I very much want to be. It is a pretty archway. In it, as if waiting for an earthquake, is my personality in bodily form. She is not real keen on the present moment, evidently, because she keeps moving from side to side, as if trying to outrun something. Anyway, in effect, she blocks my passage. I see her blocking the magic shining from the other side, so I walk up to her and consider letting her decide what I will do, but then, "Excuse me, but I need to get through." I put my hand on her shoulder— stopping her momentarily, then walk past her. As my hand has thrown off her rhythm some, she looks like one of those

ducks in a shooting gallery, gone loco. I slip off into the magic—
not feeling ecstasy, but correctness, and she, she didn't even
notice really, who I was or that I had walked by.
(End of vision)

"Mesa, that is how you take a trip and leave yourself behind,"
said Mega. "Personality is only paper with a lot of stuff written
on it. You and others wrote it, but you can always toss it and
write something new." And a new image grew in my mind as she
spoke.

Vision

In the desert, oh neverending empty empty . I ,I, I, would be a
priest, if I had a church, if I had a congregation, if I were not a
woman. I would be a priest. Directing rituals of fire and water,
anointing the believers, hanging out with the sinners—to reform
them. I have blessings to bestow...I am here with five cacti
arrayed behind me, spread out and evenly spaced, like a

candelabra on an altar. I start spinning and turn into this huge
tornado. It grows, or I do, it is kind of confusing, until I am bigger
than the whole planet and I sweep through her; cleansing her. I
am supremely centered, and when the world is clean, I become
small again, standing among the cacti.

"My work here is done."

"Good work John Wayne," Mega said, smiling. "Now I want to
remind you of some things that you have forgotten. These are
your gifts and talents, waiting to be claimed and used. To be
the woman you want to be, were intended to be, you must learn
to use your talents in service to others. That is why they were
given to you. Close your eyes." She put her palm on my
forehead and I was sitting at a table, (not really, you know, it was
a vision), with a gypsy fortune teller.

She didn't have a crystal ball—just a plate of half-eaten shrimp
fried rice and potstickers. It looked really good. She was
moving the food around on her plate with chopsticks, and pretty
nimbly too.

"What are you doing?" I ask.

"Shhh...I'm reading the rice," she says, looking at me through
black black hair with an irritated look on her face.

I thought it was great, this cross-cultural thing. Maybe a
Chinese woman somewhere was sitting in a restaurant, gazing
into a crystal ball, ordering goulash.

She then launched into a very long monologue while pulling a plate of fortune cookies closer—breaking one open at a time and reading them. She said they each told of a specific gift or talent I possessed. I was more interested in the cookies. I don't think I mentioned that I have this thing for fortune cookies. Not an addiction, just a thing. So, I was drooling.

"The cookie says you have a problem with humility, although...you have had much help from the people around you to learn this trait."

"True," I agreed, "but I don't think we need to go into a lot of detail, right?"

"Hmmm...yes, you're a little arrogant. So strange for one so...for lack of a better term, pathetically timid," she smiled.

"Oh, I don't know. I think we could have found a better term...gee, what else is in there?" leaning over the table to look at the cookie. She pulled it close to her nose and glared at me.

"The cookies say you have a kind of calm, quiet place inside that can hear plants and the natural forces of the world around you. When your sensitive nature is not being bombarded by a lot of crap."

"Really? It really says 'crap'? Can I see?"

"Would you like to do this or shall I continue?" she asked.

"Sorry. It's just a little unorthodox, don't you think, to write the word 'crap' on a fortune? They're usually so, I don't know...I've just never seen one with the word 'crap' on it."

She was staring at me, tapping the cookie on the table.

"I'm sorry. Go ahead," I said, sitting back in my chair.

She sighed and broke open another cookie. "When you know what you want, just work toward that, because you will then have it. All of the barriers that are in your way only have power to the extent that you project them in front of you."

"I'm sorry, what?" I ask.

"Things like money and dealing with the material world are very real. It's not that you're making them up, but when you get off center, in an unhappy place in your life, you get fixated on these things so that your vision is narrowed and you can no longer see the opportunities placed in your path. You also have a natural ability to receive communication from the environment around you, as well as a strong ability to radiate, to project energy in front of your path.

"When you create mentally and emotionally, it is created in the world in front of you very strongly, very quickly. It is something that everyone does, but it is a natural talent with you. When you are conscious of this gift and its applicability, you will be able to just move with the energy."

I was salivating. The cookies were just crying out to be eaten. By me.

"These are internal barriers which, by the way, are not flaws in you, that are being burned away in this process. It'll appear to come from the outside—but it is really what needs to die inside of you presenting itself."

The waiter came by with another pot of tea. I had not even noticed that there was a cup in front of me, so I drained it and poured fresh for us both. I thought if I was gracious, she might get up off some cookies. She didn't, so I was nice for no reason at all. She had a grin on one side of her mouth when she looked up at me. I hoped she wasn't reading my mind. I hate that. I don't get a chance to process stuff and sound like a better person—it's all there, in its ugly reality.

"Don't worry so much." She smiled at me. "And deal only with your own stuff. Use as a touchstone for yourself, what you really want. What your heart and gut really want. Use this as a pathway for yourself. What kinds of things make you happy? Keep coming back to that, because, the cookies say, part of your natural empowerment, which is what this whole process is about, is that you are one of the ones who can love—not in love, or 'feeling love', not like an outside force, but in the sense of BEING love. That every cell of your body is love. And you can hear that and receive that from the environment around you and very, very powerfully radiate that to the world around you. There's a part of you that looks like really wants to be of service, to the world, and this is a kind of healing work. It's very much a spiritual gift that you carry within you that will then have to be shared.

She went on, "Burn out the barriers that limit the force of love within you. It is very important for you to remember that you will really have the environment you want, once you are clear what your true goals are. Take the future, think clearly about what you want, real clearly, and then don't let that be the future. Bring it into the present. State all of those things as if they existed right now. It is a very powerful tool for you, because they will then manifest. So, remember, you do have tools to get out of feeling stuck. The problem with being stuck, besides being stuck, is that you forget what all of your tools are. Did you want to ask any questions?" she finally looked at me over a plate piled high with cookie carcasses.

"Well, are you going to throw away those cookies?" I ask.

She raised an eyebrow, so I tried to think of a better question to ask.

"I was just kidding...what I really want to know is, does that really work? I mean, I can make stuff happen myself, if I just really focus on what I want?"

"You focused on being stuck and I'd say you were pretty successful." I didn't laugh, although she did, one of those that starts out with lots of energy then winds down because it is going solo.

"It's important for you to have a sense of humor. It is a real key for you to balance and it is integral to the force of love within you. Love, forgiveness and humor are real tied in for you," she

continued, "another tool you are being given to work with is
'distance'. Stepping back from a situation as if it was someone
else and seeing the dynamics, recognizing the important issues.
Being in a situation, but not of it. Look at them from a higher
perspective. Look at them with love.

"Also," she went on, "the real relationship you want to be in, at
least from the level I am looking at, is the one between you and
yourself. Having a right relationship with yourself will then
project out in front of you with this power that you have, and the
relationship that will next be very appropriate for loving and
growing, will be there. When you are alone, it is either because
consciously or unconsciously, you have chosen to put huge
barriers up around you. There is so much love energy going on
and blossoming inside you that people will always be attracted
to you," she smiled.

"Do you think you could write that down, maybe sign it?" I ask.
"What do you really want to do? Know that it is possible, even if
everyone and everything around you is saying that it is not
possible—if you can imagine it, it can happen. It doesn't matter
what other people are saying. It can hurt, but it cannot deflect
you from your path and goal, unless you choose to get all
wrapped up in someone else's movie."

"Hmm...that's exciting." I say.

"Yes, it is. And the cookies say that being out on the Earth is
very important for you. The voices that speak to us, speak

directly from the Earth. The plants and trees, the ground, the clouds and sky, all of the life forms that are not easily perceived by the physical eyes and ears—the Deva energy. The elemental energy, the Earth, really speaks to you and you speak to her. You can give over a lot of crap..." she looked over at me, but I didn't say a word, "to the Earth. Just give it to her and let her do her transformational magic with it because it then becomes energy that pours into life. Then let love in to fill all those places that have been clogged by other things. Consecrate and bless your life in any way that you can. You have the power to bless because you are Divine."

The gypsy woman started to fade and the vision was over. I never got a damned cookie.

So, my Coyote dream says my soul-mate is on the horizon. Mega appears, tells me that I have to learn to love myself and receive love in whatever form it offers itself, then give it out to the world as a gift. And to use my imagination in service to that world. Now a gypsy woman says I have the ability to project creative energy in front of my path.

"Okay. Now what?"

GURU GOODIE:

These are elemental times, from which we are to create wholeness. A time of Alchemy: we are to take the base metals upon and with which we have built our lives, and turn them into gold. It is time to awaken the alchemists. Modern alchemy will deal with human elementals. This is the evolution of Art.

Day Four:

"Oh beloved...chocolate, cigarettes, caffeine...how I do long for
thee when I am most alone. Alak and alas, thou hast forsaken
me..." I said.

"Hey! Wake up!" Mega pops me on the forehead with a red and
white rose. I notice the colors because she has left it on my face,
between my eyes.

"Ow! Did you know there were thorns on this when you
dropped it on my face?" I asked.

"I drop nothing, oh one of ignorance...it was placed there,
precisely, and with purpose. I make few strategic errors, and
you, pining away for crap. Crap and death. Wake up and smell
the roses, Mesa."

"Gee Mega, you sound a little tense," I said, pulling a little thorn
from my chin.

"I am not tense. I am, however, ready to work. You, on the other
hand, are in withdrawal, VERY tense, and trying to pin it on
me." She said this with a look of smugness, which personally, I
find very unappealing on the faces of others. I am able to wear
this expression and it works.

"And this morning's lecture people, is 'alchemy." And she passed the water jug. I tried to wipe off a layer of sand sticking to my face and mouth with the same sandy hand that first coated my face and mouth.

"Are you awake?" She asked me.

"Does it matter? This all seems like a dream, you know what I mean?" I was grinding the sand between my teeth after every gulp of water. Hot, plastic-tasting water.

"That's a good answer. Pour some of that over your head. It'll help," she said.

"It's hot..."

"Do you always whine this much?"

"When there is someone around to whine to, yes." I answered.

"Did you say 'alchemy, alchemy, alchemy? The word feels good."

"You're right. It does feel good to say. Why do you want to lie down? How many naps do you need?"

"Mega, it takes a lot of energy to journey into virgin territory. Alchemy, AL-KEM-EE, alchemy, Alchemy, alchemy-EE, AL-chemee..."

"Okay Mesa," she said.

"alchemyalchemyalchemyalchemy..." I was totally tranced out. It was like a mantra.

"Mesa..." she picked up the rose I'd set at my side and hit me on the head.

"Hey! That thing left thorns in my face…" I had snapped out of
it.

The sensation had been interesting. The base of my throat
liked it best, like the word was springing from there. "I'm sorry,
what did you want to say about alchemy…alchemy…" I asked.

She asked me, "Do you see that one of your challenges is a
tendency to become addicted to sensation and physical
pleasure?" she wasn't smiling.

"Mega," in my most condescending tone, "how do we, how does
anyone, know, that repeating something that feels good does
not have some kind of positive effect? Maybe I am drawn to
sensation for a reason. Maybe it's a positive for me. Really
positive. For me."

"Mesa, anything loses its positive value when you become
hooked on it. Don't grasp things so tightly—they aren't going
anywhere, not really."

"How do I know that? Maybe the one time I get loose about
something, it disappears?"

"Well, I guess you don't know. You have to be loose about that
too."

"Gee, Mega, is this spirituality fun or what? I like being
enmeshed in physical stuff much more than standing solitary and
having nothing to cling to. That seems so vulnerable—
harmonicas, wind blowing through you and all that."

"Hmm...interesting argument," she said, grinning. "Are you ready to work?"

"Mega, why are we here, doing this? It's weird. You could have given me a book. Why a desert, doing imagination exercises?" I asked.

"Do you think it was a random thing that you were brought here? You were called to a purpose and you said 'yes'. Now I will help you learn to meet that commitment. Okay?" she answered.

"More visualization? I still don't get it. Why the desert?" I pushed.

"Well, the impact of a book compared to a real-life adventure...do you think the book would have had the same effect, I mean, without hitting you over the head with the book?" she asked.

"I guess I see your point. I should have brought my camera though."

"You don't need any help hanging onto things. Trust me. You chose well."

"Okay, let's go. I'm ready to work." I closed my eyes.

"Mesa, this time we need to do something a little different. I want you to talk about the echoes," she was looking at me kindly.

"What? The echoes? I don't think I can...talk about that..." I had thought it hidden from everyone but me.

"Mesa, it's okay. I was there."

"If you were there, why do you seem so healthy? I don't feel healthy. If we had the same experience, and we are the same person, wouldn't we have the same response?

Echoechoecho...that word feels good too, but I don't like the word."

"We are not the same person, or not the same person in the same expression..." she said.

"What?" I asked.

"Never mind. Look," she swept her hands between us and roses of every color were growing at our feet. I looked up at her and noticed color all around. Roses were erupting from the desert as far in every direction as I could see.

"Hey, stop. How did you do that? Did you do that? I don't like things happening that I don't understand. It makes me nervous. It's gorgeous though." I said.

"Why stop? It's lovely, isn't it?" she seemed so happy.

"Yes, it's beautiful, but I don't understand it. It's too much. How did you do that?" I asked.

"Well, I want to leave these," she pointed to the ones at our feet, "they smell nice and I think one of them likes you."

"How did you do that?"

"Alchemy," she answered, caressing one at her feet.

I reached down to touch the one wrapping itself around my calf; a yellow rose, and it had no thorns. It was perfect. The others had vanished. This one stayed until I forgot about it and then it, too, disappeared into the sand.

"Alchemy?" I asked.

"When you look at the surface of where you've come to, you see a barren place, but go beneath the surface, to the Source—to that from which all variation comes, and you will see the Life. It is the Life that you are trying to reach—the spring in the desert. And to get there, to see it, requires an act of emotional and mental alchemy. Transforming your thoughts and feelings about where you've been and where you are now. I see roses. You see sand." She put her palm on my forehead and image started to form. "Do you remember this dream?" she asked, as I closed my eyes.

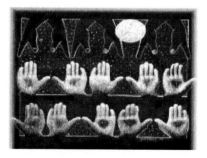

Dream:

I appeared to someone in spirit. She, the recipient, was sitting in a big overstuffed chair, asleep, a book across her knees. All of a sudden, a thousand yellow roses grow around me in the

shape of a giant horseshoe, like I just won the Kentucky Derby.
I take one of the roses and pop her on the forehead with it.

"Hey, wake up." I say, then put the rose under her nose and she
lifts her head, looks at me—not unkindly, more like I just stepped
off a spaceship.

She looked pretty friendly and up for an adventure. And since
I was winging it, it would be the same for me.

"Wanna play?" I ask her, trying at the same time to shake the
flowers, which were a bit obtrusive.

"Well, sure..." she smiles, gets up and we go outside.

"You really need to loosen up and play more..." I tell her, like I
really know what I'm talking about. We're hopping on a
hopscotch game out on a sidewalk. Then I say, "Come on," run
over to a swing set. "Watch this," I say, swinging harder and
higher until I am even with the top of the bar. Then I turn into an
eagle and fly off to an immense forest on top of a ring of
mountains that just appeared in front of us. "Now, you do it," I
say, and she does.

Anyway, we fly to the top of these two fir trees and take a look
around. She's looking kind of dazed, but smiling, being a good
sport.

I take off into the air, clean air, and she follows me. We fly to her
house, which is conveniently very close by. All that's in her
house is a bedroom and a fireplace, like props in a play. I think

to myself, "Gee, I wonder what Freud would make of this dream," but decide not to let that ruin my good time and let it go. I look over at her bed because I notice there is something square and black in the center of it. It turns into smoke as I walk over, and starts getting really intense—filling the room and threatening to engulf me. I get panicky for a moment, then say, "No," and it turns into a black suitcase and I shove it off the bed, to the floor.

"What was that?" she asks me.

"I don't know...maybe Freud, but excess baggage anyway."

"Really? Well, thanks, really. I haven't been able to sleep in the center of my bed forever."

"Oh sure, no problem." I felt like the Lone Ranger. "Well, I have stuff to do," I finally say, having exhausted all fantasies of myself as a hero.

"Yeah, me too," she says, "thanks for coming."

"Sure, see ya." I walk off—no cape, no mask or great looking boots. Just me. A cape would have been nice, though. I knew I was doing something important—smoke is not always a good thing to find in your bed—but it would have been nice if someone could see by my outfit that I was doing something important.

Mega rubs my forehead and I open my eyes. "Hmm...I do remember that. Who was she?" I asked.

"Doesn't matter. What does matter is why you went and what you did there. There is need for you to clear your own bed of excess baggage. It is, in fact, an alchemical opportunity." She was chewing a piece of dead straw and it looked pretty good. I was really hungry.

"Can I have some of that?" I asked, reaching for the straw.

"It's the only one I have...oh, alright, if you're going to drool." She forked it over.

"Thanks. Hey, did you give me the end you already chewed? It's soggy...and Mega, my bed IS clear. Clear as the Sahara, as a matter of fact. Have you looked around? Trust me, it is no different at home."

"Oh? You mean hot and sandy?" she smiled.

"No, that is not what I meant..." I considered putting more effort into steering her toward my self-pity, but knew she'd never play along.

"Gee, I'm sorry. It must be rough—how do you manage?" she was still smiling and annoying the hell out of me.

"Anyway..." I sulked. She had a real talent for making me feel like I was twelve or thirteen years old.

"Hey, let's have a fire." She turned around, moving her hands in space, somehow drawing flames up from the very ground, which was hot, but not nearly aflame just a moment before.

"Gee, Mega, you do a lot of useful things. Is that a real fire? Any hotdogs?" I stuck my hand in it, burning myself.

"This is a good time for you, for us. The pause between reels; sunset. Have you noticed an affinity for dusk? How do you feel right now?" She asked.

"Right now...I love the color of they sky. It's almost turquoise. It seems magical and reminds me of that painting by Rousseau, 'The Sleeping Gypsy'. It's like...the expansiveness of the color moves through my body, opening my lungs. You know, sometimes I hear dusk calling to me. Is that weird? I can be doing something pretty engrossing and then comes this really quiet voice, 'Mesa, it's time. Come out, come out.' It's like a friend you have known forever, but rarely get to see, and when you do, there is no need to talk—that familiar, you know?"

"Hmm, I like that. Go on," she said, laying back on the sand and closing her eyes. We both listened to the crackling fire for a moment, and then I went on, with my eyes closed.

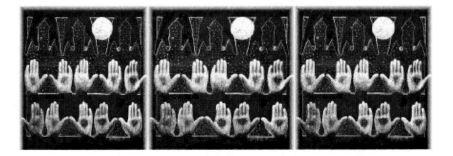

"Go on, okay, dusk, sundown...I feel like dancing. I'm fluid, and it's private. I want to dance alone, but I'm not really alone. The air has body. I almost feel as though I could rise and fly and the air would hold me up. I always feel that way at night. In the silence; when everyone is sleeping and dreaming and creating new worlds, where we are not bound.

Moths fly through the air, moonlight on their wings. They come to me and they are so still when they land like the center of something that could blow you apart if you lost your balance there. And I like that. It means I have to be totally awake. And at night, I feel like I can turn sideways and slip into a crack in the sky or Earth and disappear. The world is different after the sun goes down. There is a resonance, you know, like the last vibration of a stricken gong. I don't hear it, but I feel it. So, yes, I feel an affinity for dusk—it's a doorway to all the magic."

"So, you don't feel like you're hiding or anything like that? At night—you don't prefer it because you can easily fade into the dark?" she asked.

"Hiding? From what?"

"People, the past."

"Oh, the things that happened to me when I was a kid, usually, almost always, took place at night. If I was going to hide, wouldn't I be more likely to avoid being alone with those memories at night? I embrace the night. And I don't avoid people at night—that's when I'm most comfortable. I think it's my element."

"True."

"I don't know what it is, this draw to the dark, but I feel very connected to life, real life, there—to light, like I am illuminated strongly in the dark, or not afraid to look in there or something. It's kind of thrilling because it's a mystery after a certain point—you know?" I continued. "There are memories of night that feed me as well as those that prey on me."

"Tell me about one that feeds you..." she said, eyes still closed.

"Okay. Well, I remember this...sitting on a park bench across the street from my apartment. There is an assertive breeze—not quite bullying, but I had to take notice. It is laying out my hair in opposing directions. Cars are going by in front of me. It's not quite dark, but everything wears its shadow out front, so you cannot be sure, or absolutely certain of anything. It was exciting. The movement of air—messing with my hair, the cool damp grass under my bare feet, the drone of cars going by, the sprinklers on in the background, the clouds packed up and grouped like they were taking off for awhile all together, my own hands not solid lines. I was nearly invisible, and I knew; I had a solid awareness, that everything could completely alter while I blinked. There was no solidity, no intense lighting like midday.

And I was so full of this—the aroused air, the sprinklers rattling like snakes, the grass teasing my skin...I couldn't feel lonely...touched by so much. The air knows us better than any lover and making love should always feel that close and impossible to hold onto. I wanted to shake out of my skin, and feel the wind move through me all night. I mean, we have these wonderful bodies with skin, to be touched and moved, but there is all this space between our cells that we never explore.

So, I just threw out my arms, fingered the air, embraced the wind, and said, 'this is for you...I give myself to you, completely.' I was kind of embarrassed afterward though, like it made me seem a little pathetic to be so...grateful...to a lover, but really, it felt so good."

Mega smiled and turned over on her side, facing me. "Mmm...I remember that. It was very good." And I felt self-conscious immediately, forgetting that I was talking to myself, so I smiled at Mega. "It's nice, you know, having my favorite Myself to talk with. I'm curious, do you think there is anything wrong with loving, or falling in love, well...with yourself? I just wonder, because I have never felt this way about anyone, certainly not myself, like everything is really okay, even good, when we are together." I couldn't believe I was embarrassed by this, but I was. She smiled. The moon pulled closer and the stars bent in, listening. "It's elemental..." she said quietly, and the air moved between us. I closed my eyes as a gentle movement of air—a whisper at my neck, warm breath wrapping round—slid across my lips, blessed my eyes. Fingering my hair, lifting every strand, joining ends, forming tracery. Feather kisses on my skin tickled and made me laugh. It was a filigree of touch; openwork—I felt precious for the first time in my life. As fire rose in my body, a cold wave of clamoring echoes pushed through from the furthest civilization of my body where they had long been exiled. They rose and then fell before this private miracle; my healing.

I remembered conception and love in the dark. "Beloved," whispered the air.

Day Five:

When I awoke, there was a twitch of orange at the horizon as the sun tried to come up. I embraced the night, giving my thanks. We die in sleep and it is so light, this dusting, that we miss it; a fine layer beneath the scenery.

There are still a few stars out. They are pretty quiet, though they want very much to talk. (You know these things with intimates.) There is a note, I had to laugh, next to my pillow of sand. It was from Mega.

"Beloved"

awake, north wind

and come, south wind!
blow on my garden
    that it's fragrance may spread
       abroad.
let my lover come into my garden
    and taste its choice fruits.

"Lover"

I have come into my garden, my
    sister, my bride.

"Friends"

Eat, O friends, and drink
    drink your fill, O lovers.

(Song of Solomon

Holy Bible, Zondervan)

Love, Mega
(p.s. you slept in the middle of your bed last night.)

The stars just couldn't keep it in any longer—came rushing down, danced on the ends of my fingers. Danced, danced, we all danced. And there was a voice, a whisper dancing around my head, and words formed:

"To the Universe belongs the dancer. He who does not dance does not know what happens. Now if you follow my dance, see yourself in Me who am speaking—you who dance, consider what I do, for yours is this passion of man which I am to suffer."

(Jesus to his followers
Acts of John,
Gnostic text)

I stopped dancing, looked around for a body attached to the voice. "I've never heard that before. Mega, where are you?"
"I'm here."

"Where? Why don't I see you? And why are you whispering?" I
could barely hear her, what with a desert full of dancing stars.
You know how they can be.

"Sssh...guys. I can't hear," I tell them.

They rose together, in one white mass and it was quite lovely.

"Anyway, Mega?"

"Yes?"

"I'd like to see you." I was looking silly, going in a slow circle,
searching for her body, following her voice.

"You have," she laughed, but in a whisper, so she sounded like
dead leaves rubbing together.

"Just listen to my voice, as big as you can. Listen big and listen
round," she said.

"Gee, cryptic, really..." I was still moving in circle. It was weird,
how my body seemed drawn to circle. It became more interesting
than chasing a voice so I stopped doing that and just let myself
follow myself.

After a few minutes of this, I was apparently burrowing into the
Earth because I found myself knee deep in a hole, but I could
not stop. I felt pulled to circle. Dancing in a circle, me and
Mega, embracing, spinning in space. I, no, we, are digging a large
crater in the Earth. Looks like we're in Arizona, by the color of
the surrounding hills whizzing by.

Anyway, we are burrowing deeper, deeper, deeper, creating a very direct route to the center of the Earth. I feel pretty happy—complete and everything. Right as we get to the center of the Earth, I am alone and there is a large fire. Around this fire sit several people with blankets on. This is a large cave and I am not sure what to do with myself. No one looks at me, although a person to my left is the only one I clearly notice. I figure, in a humble kind of way, I can do pretty much anything since this is my vision, so I thank them for letting me come, and I just walk over and step into the fire. I think anyone would have done the same. It was interesting. I could really breathe; my lungs felt totally clear.

Then I heard a pulse, a drum or something. And a voice...it calls me back to the desert. So I thank everyone for letting me stand in the fire. It was the best bath I have ever had. I then walk through a crack in the wall of the cave, and find myself lying flat out on the sand, still slowly spinning, but the cave is gone. I open my eyes and the sky is dark except for a blaze of stars looking back at me. I am losing track of time. Losing myself.

GURU GOODIE:
"Throw your past upon the fire and warm yourself today. You can do nothing with now, when your hands are full of then."

Day Six:

Before opening my eyes, voices quietly call over the sand; whispers skipping across the crystals, like dust on a stream of light--An intricate pattern of feathered sound. When I feel lonely, I seek pattern; there I can satisfy expectation, like a weaving into which I can nestle and be protected from chaos.

Last night's dream:

I am atop an ocean of black, and content to stay for a while.
There appears to be a flicker, a ripple, a rise and a flash of light
across the flat black sea: the body of black has risen. Wing to
wing, silent as nothing, hurting my ears, was a mass of ravens.
Their wings, afire with brilliant ice light, nearly blind me.
Only just realizing I have no body, I too rise and find my current
of air. The ravens precede me, so I see only black, hear only
nothing. We are in no hurry—an eternity of no fear—so big, this
lack of fear. There is music. Then a voice comes out of
nowhere, flying through the black, right up in my face. "Wake up,
the Universe is dancing to its own heartbeat. You must rise and
dance. The dancer in your heart is calling you. Catch the air, it
is moving. Wake up!"
The voice had no body to back up its pushiness, but it was right.
The Universe was really going at it and the mood was too good
to ignore. I felt more alive than I'd ever felt before, ever.
Electric. Then I noticed a curious, urgent thrumming beneath
this joy. It was like a chant, or a spiritual and there were shadows
and shades of sound, passing before me there in the air.
The voice from the black, a woman's voice, spoke again: "These
are the religious—silent men, women, and children, altogether—a
collective sound, that cannot be heard. It has no voice, just a
pulse. All of them separate in body, chanting alone in cloistered

lives; joyless celibates—a cacophony of thwarted spirit. I knew
this sound of which she spoke. It had been my own.

"This sound—shadow within shadowed doorways, dark within
darkened windows, the vibration that lifts a song to the range of
our listening, pushes gospel up to our collective hearing. The
silent ones sing subterranean currents of heart—
excommunicated monks and nuns in communities of one, in a
world network of parts incomplete—connected by this silence.
Just under the surface only, because deeply within, this heart
sound gathers momentum and is finding voice, ready to burst
through the surface of life, like sea creatures dreaming of wings
and waking in mid-flight.

And the voice from the black, that I now knew to be Mega, said
to me, "Mesa, you can free this voice by giving it your ear."

"Really? You mean like Vincent Van Gogh?"

"Listen Mesa, and give this sound its voice."

So I listened, I really tried, and then I heard it myself, starting to
take form in my ears. It had once been my own, but now a choir
filled my ears, and it hurt. It was so large.

The dream faded back to black and I woke to Mega's voice.

"Your echoes, Mesa, are incomplete sounds from the past and
part of the silence that deafens our world. Join the chorus and
sing your new song—our new song."

It must have been a very long dream…it was now the very late side of day six.
I think the seventh day is one of rest.

Day Seven:

I had an amazing day. I've been writing everything down. I haven't eaten in days and all of my thoughts sound so, I don't know, like they belong to someone else. Like my voice dropped an octave or I'm in slow motion. Like I am becoming someone else.

I don't feel like doing anything but being here; emptying out and letting the stuff fall on the page. Writing it down is the only way I'll remember any of this, or believe it actually happened.

Anyway, when I woke this morning, I was feeling like it's almost time to go back home. An ending is here, and a beginning just as clearly.

And now, induced by hunger, no doubt, vision is trying to take form behind my eyes.

Vision:

My two feet...I look at them and see a faint light fall across my toes. Off to the right, out there in the heart of the desert—I've been here long enough now to be familiar with her body—under the rays of the moon, was a glowing object. Some kind of vase, or a chalice, I think. I wasn't sure it was solid—it could have been a mirage, but the sun was not yet up. What the hell, I figured, and got up to walk over for a closer look. It seemed to be full of water, but strange water—infused with light. And I could see all the way through the inside when I leaned over it, and out into space on the other side. I mean outer space, the Universe. It reminded me of when I was a kid and I wanted to dig a hole in the backyard, all the way to China. I had always believed that idea and now I had proof. Definitely, China could be gotten to through this hole.

I picked up the chalice to look underneath, but there was only sand, so I set it back down. This was curious. I squatted down next to it--just waited for it to speak to me in some fashion, and finally, it did.

"Come on, you know you want to. Jump in," said Mega.

"What?" I asked.

"Dive in," she said.

"Well, okay." And I did. I thought I'd get to see China and everything in between. I'd reach the depths, pass through to the other side and emerge into space.

"You do not reach the depths, Mesa. As water, you are the depths," she said.

"Am I water then?" I asked without benefit of mouth, because indeed, I had become water.

I went with the flow, there being one. It went around in a spiral, and it felt like dancing with no legs. Anyway, I saw a pinpoint of light far beyond, and flowed toward it. As I approached, I saw it was an opening into moonlight and I was soon to be part of a major waterfall that would cascade over my desert. I was terrified for a moment—not that it made a bit of difference, since I could not stop this movement.

After falling through space, myself a million drops of water, like cells exploding in the air, I came crashing down upon the desert in a monumental spray—myself unloosed upon the Earth. Sweeping through the dust, spread out and yet whole, pulling up greenery behind me. You should have heard the desert's gratitude. It was really singing.

I had come home, and not really gone anywhere at all. I lay there in liquid body, enjoying my new self. "This is something you don't do every day," I thought to myself. Then as I pulled myself together and sprang to my feet—an eager meeting with life—I caught my reflection under the moon. "Hey!" the reflection was not mine.

It was Mega. I was Mega. Okay, I already knew this, but she was Out There, Down the Road, in the Future. I hadn't been here long enough to call this day a real future. To what? Six days ago? Did that really qualify as a past? It seemed pretty sudden. Maybe time moves faster out here, having nothing to block its path.

"Wait, Mega...I miss you, having you to talk to and look at. At least when I could look at you, it was like real company. Now I am back talking to myself." She was now so close, we could talk in whisper. And she answered, "This will help you to remember to look inside first. If you want to see me, look in a mirror. If you want to talk, go within."

I don't know why this made me sad. It was almost mourning, this feeling. Things were different now. Something was gone. A new thing was here, and I needed time to get used to this intimacy. That hole that I'd been carrying around with such resignation had been filled, and I felt kind of robbed.

This was so much to process, that I felt like being alone for awhile—away from people and everything else. Fortunately, I was alone in the heart of a desert. (Boy, this synchronicity. This kind Universe.) I walked back to my impression in the sand that I had called home for the past week, to be alone in a different spot than the one I had just been standing on a moment before. There were distinct differences in quality between the two, and among the infinity of other choices, I chose my old impression.

A weird thing happened though. I didn't like my old impression anymore. It didn't feel right, didn't support me as it had in the past, just moments ago. Didn't feel like home. Yet, sitting there, everything looked the same as it had the past few days. In a desert, where things are known for their reliability, except for when it rains, except for many things, but never mind, this was not okay. Too old, too the same. I had to move. Maybe I'll make an impression elsewhere, maybe not; maybe I'll just walk around, stay mobile—check out the view on the move. The land is big—I'll go somewhere new. Maybe I'll dance. I have a partner now. An eternity of we.

And I must have been sending out some great vibes, because I noticed, on the outskirts of my normal attention, creatures coming closer in. They didn't approach me, they were, okay, this is going to be hard to believe, but they were dancing. Seriously.

Out there, beyond me, birds and beautiful animals of all sizes
and makeup, dancing in circles. Many circles, inside one
another, from wide and slow--in, to smaller and a little faster, all
the way to the center circle of three going by in a blur. Like
cogs. Their circles moved with my circle of one. There must
have been seven or eight circles of them, every one moving in the
same direction. Every creature was doing this dance--a graceful
thing, sort of different from one to another, whatever came
naturally to body type or temperament, but all the same spirit,
really. We all looked related in purpose, so you cold call it a
group movement. And it was so outlandish and impossible to
ignore, you'd think Busby Berkeley was behind the scenery
somewhere.

Anyway, we're all trying to be respectful, you know, everyone
doing their own thing, but mindful of the group's union of motion
though the purpose of the dance was not yet clear. I thought,
"Gee, this is great..." I could feel a beat coming up through my
feet. I tried to let it move me because it felt more graceful than
my body. So, I surrendered to its integrity and flow, but I had to
look once in awhile. It was a new experience for me, and I wanted
to remember everything. I wouldn't, I knew. Details are too
untidy sometimes and so usually ignored, but I wanted to grasp
the colors, the big movements, the sounds and aromas. Like at a
circus, no, circuses are depressing. This dance had great
creature dignity. They were magnificent. Birds with translucent

wings, rainbow plummeage—feathers that carried dancing stars upon them, (stars insist on being a part of everything), yellows that made me really thirsty; reds that pushed deep into my heart like my own blood; greens that gave me hope. Hope—green was the one—the key; the color that started a vision. The animals, the creatures now too had closed their collective eyes and I did as well. We all moved in unison, dipped and spun, spread our limbs—our extensions, in slow-motion over the sand, feet assertive in the production of this dance—creation, I think.

Vision:

Green baby trees; saplings, poked through the sand at our feet. And in groups, like families born together, green plants pushed up and waved at the new sky. Born dancing, moving in spirals up from the Earth—circling gracefully between our circles. The greenery sprang up and swelled, filling the desert. Soon, the air was full of moisture, and when I pulled it deeply into my lungs, I heard the whales. Green grew there among us. The virginity of this creation made me cry. This dance, our dance, a collective effort, wove colors across the desert; brought us together and held us fast. I didn't feel out of place with the others, which was a new thing—an idea I hadn't yet happened upon. A partnership of creation.

The dance exhausted me, all of us, but no one stopped. They didn't so I couldn't shame my own species. And we were truly creating—growing life right up from the Earth, with our rhythms. When we danced slowly, we created slower things—mountains and rocks. Faster movements bore things of air streaking across the sky. We were working hard, but it was a labor of love. Worlds can be built in a day. I know. We did it. We created a new one, all of us. And when we were so tired that we barely moved, though our fatigue still pulled us in spiral, (all things growing and releasing that way) we had given birth to the Earth and she held us to her when we finally laid down together to sleep, and to dream.

(end of vision)

I know...this stuff sounds pretty hokey, but visions are like that. And deep down in the very center of every person on the planet is a spot of hokey. For some it is small, and others seem to embody it fully, but it is there and it is the part of ourselves that calls up these visions—to see what we truly want.

We send our visions out into the world in some form, always, always we are changed somehow by these gifts, and if orphaned out in the world, they land where they may with lives of their own.

If we are good parents to our visions, we grow them up until they can live independently, healthily.

This dance, my meeting at heart and mind with the Life of Earth, was lovely and that in itself has changed me. I cannot help but carry it within me now, that sacredness. Sacred simply because beauty, harmony and grace embodied, even for the length of a single dance, is Divine. Holy.

Later in the Seventh Day:

Choosing another impression—in the still warm sand, legs and arms drawn up, the sun has gone down and moon will soon arrive. Thoughts kick around like tics of overtired muscles. I think about going back to the world. I think...I think...I think, I think, I think...the word sounds so metallic. "Think", I think, you think, we think...sounds like a robot with a limp. Anyway, I think I see in the blue-gray shimmering air around the distant orange hills, a camel carrying a Beduoin man. Boy, these desert people. I love what he's wearing. I could wear that.

Funny thing about deserts; the heat, the flat, the empty, the strange animals that populate them, including us, the great tans, the religious symbolism. I think all of creation begins here. Maybe it really is only the heat...a kiss is a kiss, even if it is a dry pucker.

GURU GOODIE:
"Now, go ye forth, be fruitful,
and do not divide."

Leaving:

When I woke up, it was so quiet, I could hear my own breathing, my own heart. I could hear the rotation of the Earth, the sparkle of stars, although they have toned down their brilliance—their dialogue simple and soft-spoken.

I can hear the sand moving, although a low sweeping breeze has tucked most sound in its pocket as it passes. The light has dimmed and softened, with no edges, like a candle's flame under frosted glass. The cacti have pulled in their needles—no damage, no repair. Kindness. They give only their slow, steady green.

The air covers me in thin blankets, nudges me to move closer to my Mother, my bed, myself. So, I wrap myself gently within my own arms, knowing I am mother to myself when I leave this place and need to practice while still in the presence of my Teacher. This trip—my death, my rebirth, it's been a quiet thing. I have come home to my body. Been gone so long, I was afraid I would forget my native language, but the body remembers. I finally have been born whole within this culture; our experiment.

I rested.

On the road home:

A prayer—
"Forgive me, when in my own pain, I have wounded another. When my emotional limping has tripped others as I made my own way. And thank-you, Sacredness-In-All, (feeling magnanimous), for teaching me to walk evenly on two legs. Had

you not given me the seed, I would not have grown the leg that earlier you took from under me."

I practiced this prayer on my way home this morning, feeling purposeful, although I could not have explained this purpose. Not clearly, anyway. Walking along the highway, I caught sight of Coyote, off to the right. She ran through the sagebrush, up close and stopped. Then she laughed. "Well?" she asked. "Tell them, tell them I spoke the Truth," she said, grinning. I am telling you now. I threw her a mighty sweet kiss as she ran off in the direction from which she'd just come—over the sand, toward the hills. She turned suddenly and I saw that she had just caught it, my kiss, and was rubbing it all over herself. "I bet they just don't get enough of that," I said to myself.
I was glad to give her something she could use.
As for me, I was full alive in my skin—ready to touch the world. I wanted to unfold in the world like the flower I had seen blooming alone in the desert. She had taught me about singularity of vision, and perseverance. One grows. One knows nothing else naturally. We often miss these quiet lessons spoken mouth against ear, but not this time. I was grateful. Even my pores were breathing and singing my thanks. The Earth hears these songs, believe it.
And I am in perpetual embrace: Mega within me now; complete. Embodied. To my left, in early morning sunlight, a wishing star

raced over me, paused above the hills that lay up against this highway, waved to us all here on Earth, and brilliant as she was, cast herself down in a huge display of light in the desert. The sky, knowing full well the truth about life and death, lit a small candle right there over the desert, only for a moment, in remembrance. And then there was joy—singing and dancing. Stars hold the secret of the Dance. I listened very big, very round, as I had been taught, and heard the star who gave herself up:

LESSON TWO:

"Mesa, give yourself away in a blaze of light. Love the hell out of the world."

Her words pointed down the same road I was on, but to a different journey—a new one. Bigger. I had to look at the road before me with different eyes. The air there on the side of the highway swirled around me, pulling my head up to look at the sky, as my body dug down deep to find the right rhythm. My arms, so prone now to fly themselves, reached full out in the air, looking

for the lift that would take us higher. I circled for the longest
time, when I noticed a lightness to my body.
Spinning in circle, just inches above the road, I felt something
within take form, body moving within me—like cream into butter; a
new form. I was light and offered myself as a gift to the star and
to the sky that nurtured them all until they gave themselves away.
You just have to say thank-you when you are given a gift. You
must.

Ω

"now, go ye forth, be fruitful, and do not divide."
--Goddess

GURU GOODIE:
"Wilderness is not disappearing. We have only to close our eyes to be swallowed up by the untame."

Epilogue:

Ten years ago, I was looking for wilderness. Constraints of time and responsibility did not allow a long trek into the middle of nowhere, so I looked closer in. the original plan was to get myself to the center of a desert and take my chances on fate. What I settled for was the top of a sand dune in between an RV park and a 7-Eleven two blocks away. On my way, I found wilderness in many forms: the side of a road, a stranger's company, my own mind.

I walked into Moses Lake, Washington, the town whose name I had just found the night before. It had been irresistible, that name, standing to attention on the map as I ran my fingers along the colored lines of highway and road. Moses Lake...what better place to begin a spiritual quest—a symbolic journey into the wilderness. Moses, the prophet...I took the name as a sign, the bad or good of which was not yet clear. It just seemed symbolic of something, and therefore, significant.

My mind was beginning to cramp with the intricate weaving and reweaving of endless signs and symbols in the design of my life. I tried to follow the thread, even when it became entangled with another's and I mistook it for my own. I needed that thread—it had brought me here or I had carried it; it had crossed the path of this place where the tension slipped and that was reason enough to stop.

Alone in this wilderness, atop my sand dune, I surveyed the wild. Beasts sprang from the shadows in my mind. I was alone here, left only with hunger. The dictionary defines wilderness as a region uncultivated and uninhabited by human beings: waste—an empty or pathless region. For all intents and purposes, this was an empty place, and I filled it with wanting. I wanted; deeper, fuller, higher, wider—more. I wanted much more in my life, needed more of life. So I stood on this dune and tried to consume the emptiness. The sand dune wasn't very high, but elevated enough to make the rest of the world look just a bit smaller, simpler to form into a clear and manageable picture. I pulled a small hip flask of Amaretto from my pocket and slid down on the dune. The liquor was warm and sweet, like the rain that had started to sprinkle the sand. I let it take me back to a familiar place, where a friend was telling me of her need to go to Death Valley and wrestle with her soul. I wondered then, and now, why she, or any of us, would want to wrestle with our souls when an embrace is infinitely more gentle.

Embracing my own embattled soul, I lay back on the sand and closed my eyes to sleep, the wind rumpling my hair like a lover. I trekked through the wilderness of my own mind for a week here and came back to town like a hermit thrust into a conversation with a world she had succeeded in muting, if only for a time.

We can get lost in the wilderness because no one has blazed a trail there. Within, the wild place is waiting to take us in, temper us in the fire of unnamed desires and needs, to make us sure-footed in dense undergrowth. We are the Outback. We are the Aborigines. We have just wandered off together into dangerous civilization. We can always go home.

We can always go out and find wilderness in the shape of desert, forest, mountain, and sea, but the distance from civilization takes us not a step closer to our true destination; the landscape of our souls, where we live as natives.

—Mesa Doe

About the Author

Author, **Mesa Doe**, Near-Holywoman, lives in New Mexico.
mesadoe@earthlink.net

Artist Sharon Fernleaf lives in Albuquerque, New Mexico.
She co-owns Near-Holy p r e s s with Sherri Roberts,
publishing "spirituality with a smile"—books on self-empowerment,

Ω

About Near-Holy Books(tm):

These are the inspired writings of everyday Teachers, as told
to Mesa Doe, Near-Holywoman. As a set, they comprise the
Near-Holy Bible (tm).

Near-Holy

p r e s s

2134 Metzgar Road SW
Albuquerque, New Mexico 87105
c/o Sharon Fernleaf and Sherri Roberts,

If you have any feedback on this story, please feel free to write
or email: mesadoe@earthlink.net

ORDER FORM

Near-Holy Press
2134 Metzgar Road SW
Albuquerque, New Mexico 87105
Phone: 505-452-9599

Please send a copy of The Way of Doe. I understand that I may return it for a full refund—for any reason, no questions asked. ($12.00 plus shipping and handling)

Name: _____

Address: _____

City: _____ State: _____ Zip: _____

Telephone: _____ Email: _____

Shipping by air: US $4.00 first book, $2.00 each additional.
International: $9.00 for first book; $5.00 each additional.
Sales Tax: Please add 5.8% for books shipped to New Mexico addresses.